Strategy
In A Week

Stephen Berry

Stephen Berry is a former CFO, an international MBA lecturer in Business Strategy and author of *Strategies of the Serengeti*, which applies the successful strategies of the East African animal residents of the Serengeti to business. The book has been sold in over 100 countries and Stephen's business conference speeches on these strategies have been delivered in 25 countries across four continents. He has also trained many executives in strategic thinking and assisted a wide variety of organizations by facilitating sessions to generate their strategies. Stephen is passionate about making strategy practical, understandable and successful.

Teach® Yourself

Strategy In A Week

Stephen Berry

First published in Great Britain in 2012 by Hodder Education

This edition published in 2016 by John Murray Learning

Copyright © Stephen Berry 2012, 2016

The right of Stephen Berry to be identified as the Author of the Work has been asserted by him in accordance with the Copyright, Designs and Patents Act 1988.

Database right Hodder & Stoughton (makers)

The *Teach Yourself* name is a registered trademark of Hachette UK.

British Library Cataloguing in Publication Data: a catalogue record for this title is available from the British Library.

ISBN 9781473610347

eISBN 9781473622319

1

The publisher has used its best endeavours to ensure that any website addresses referred to in this book are correct and active at the time of going to press. However, the publisher and the author have no responsibility for the websites and can make no guarantee that a site will remain live or that the content will remain relevant, decent or appropriate.

The publisher has made every effort to mark as such all words which it believes to be trademarks. The publisher should also like to make it clear that the presence of a word in the book, whether marked or unmarked, in no way affects its legal status as a trademark.

Every reasonable effort has been made by the publisher to trace the copyright holders of material in this book. Any errors or omissions should be notified in writing to the publisher, who will endeavour to rectify the situation for any reprints and future editions.

Typeset by Cenveo® Publisher Services.

Printed and bound in Great Britain by CPI Group (UK) Ltd., Croydon, CR0 4YY.

John Murray Learning policy is to use papers that are natural, renewable and recyclable products and made from wood grown in sustainable forests. The logging and manufacturing processes are expected to conform to the environmental regulations of the country of origin.

John Murray Learning
Carmelite House
50 Victoria Embankment
London EC4 0DZ
www.hodder.co.uk

Contents

Introduction

For most aspiring managers, at some point in their careers, their Personal Development Plans will include the demand to have 'greater strategic thinking ability'. We have the perception that executives operating at board-level have this 'strategic thinking ability' but seldom find the route to obtain it for ourselves. The purpose of this book is to provide that route. Strategy, like any other discipline, can be learned and practised. This book takes the reader on a journey to explore what organizational strategy is, where it fits within the context of each business, and then gives an examination of internal, external, marketing, brand and competitive strategy.

To progress to an executive position, a wide range of skills and attributes are required. Aspects such as good leadership skills, strong communication skills, commercial understanding and the ability to understand other people are all needed. Equal with these vital elements is the ability to have a good grasp of strategic thinking.

Good strategic thinking is at a huge premium in business. Far too often we see elementary errors made by very highly paid executives who undoubtedly should know better. We see businesses with successful niche products try to expand beyond their niche and then realize that it was a gargantuan error. We see successful companies stumble due to an inability to see threats or opportunities. We see companies over-expanding within their market and wondering why they trip over. The business history books are littered with organizations that supposedly exhibited a degree of 'excellence', but failed; companies who were supposedly 'built to last' but clearly weren't; companies who were supposedly moving from 'good to great' but the leveller of time has consigned them to mediocrity or even collapse.

The American company Levi Strauss was the original manufacturer of denim jeans – they had 100 per cent of the market. They decided that they were not niche jeans suppliers, but that they were 'clothing manufacturers'. That expansion and the failure to deal with entrants to the jeans market meant that by 2010 their 100 per cent market share had eroded to a mere 10 per cent.

The German company Mercedes-Benz were the executive saloon car of choice for many business people. The ownership of this aspirational iconic vehicle was, at one point, a sign of career success. By spreading themselves throughout the market with a range of comical vehicles such as the A-class, B-class, M-class and R-class, for many executives, they have lost their aspirational qualities and manufacturers such as Jaguar, owned by Indian firm Tata, are benefiting by filling this gap.

The Royal Bank of Scotland became preoccupied with expansion and failed to note the warnings evident when it was negotiating with Dutch bank ABN-AMRO. This merger contributed to the failure of the bank, which was subsequently rescued by the British taxpayer in much the same way that American Insurance Group (AIG) was rescued by the American taxpayer. The taxpayers are now the owners of failed businesses who did not get their strategies right.

In this book we will explore failures and successes, and we will provide the platform for the reader to acquire the vital skills of strategic thinking.

SUNDAY

Understand what strategy is and what it isn't

People mean different things when they use the word 'strategy'. It is easy to define linguistically – from two Greek words 'stratos' (army) and 'ago' (to lead) and as such is about 'leading armies'. However, that is not a useful definition for business – the military analogy, as we shall see later, is mostly an unhelpful analogy. Strategy has often developed a mystique of something that is achieved by highly intelligent beings in the boardroom contemplating things so difficult to imagine that those outside the boardroom simply would not understand. This too is unhelpful. Strategy is simple. It is about establishing where you want to be and planning to get there. This chapter unpacks some of the myths of strategy and outlines some of the varying meanings people put to the word. To be an effective strategic thinker, we need to avoid the myths and 'speak' each of these meanings fluently, with the ability to move between them at ease. These 'meanings' are all strategy – they are all the right answer – so, do not choose between them; understand them all.

For both the myths and the meanings, I will use ideas already available. The myths will be drawn from those in my book *Strategies of the Serengeti* and the various meanings will be my adaptations of those used by Henry Mintzberg *et al.* in *Strategy Safari*. So, with an African theme to our journey (journey is 'safari' in Swahili and the Serengeti is a vast plain spanning much of Tanzania and Kenya), let us firstly consider what strategy is not.

Strategy is not military

Much of our business terminology has military roots from the title of 'Chief Executive Officer', to taking holiday being referred to as 'going on leave'. Strategy has a military definition – the combining of the words 'stratos' and 'ago'. However, a military focus to business strategy would be disastrous. The military focus is on defeating the enemy. In business, the focus is on profitably satisfying the customers' needs. Treating the customer as the enemy would not yield a business that lasts!

Any military option has an end – victory. In business, ongoing success is the aim. Strategy aims for long-term survival and longevity, not a single definitive 'victory' end point.

Military operations have a limited sphere of activity – even the world wars did not encompass the entire world. Business can choose to limit itself or can choose to be globally omnipresent. The sphere of activity is not limited to geography. There is no rule in business that prevents a timber company from making rubber boots, then rubber cables, then the wires within cables, then telecommunications, then mobile phones (US: cell phones). We know the above company now as the Finnish giant Nokia – the military analogy would have been too limiting for their success.

Some military analogies and terminology can be useful, so do not cast them aside. However, the overarching framework of strategy is that it is much bigger, longer lasting and much more widely encompassing than the military aspects often used to describe strategy.

Strategy is not only for the hyper-intelligent

Perhaps this is a myth that is too flattering for executives to seek to defuse – although some of the decisions mentioned in this book will undoubtedly question the wisdom of some executives, albeit with the benefit of hindsight. When an organizational role includes 'strategic responsibilities', it is sometimes set apart as of greater worth and requiring higher calibre than tactical or operational responsibilities. As we shall see in the next chapter, all aspects – strategic, tactical and operational – are required for success and each is equally punctuated by potential business minefields.

We all do strategy. Perhaps part of your reason for reading this book is to understand strategy and develop your strategic thinking ability – that in itself is something that is part of your personal strategy of increasing business skills, presumably with the aim of career advancement or the success of your own business. Your very reading of this book is therefore an act with strategic intent.

Strategy is equally applicable to the global giant and the sole trader. One very smart business strategist I know left school with negligible qualifications and runs a hairdressing shop in the UK Midlands. He has steered it very successfully with a strong understanding of the customers (generally older clientele), the market (they want consistency and the same stylist as they had the previous week), the competitors (who are often seeking to be fashionable or trying something new), his distinct offering to the market (a strand of consistency for his customers in an ever accelerating world) and appreciation of his competitive advantage (i.e. what he does better than competitors – recognising his customers' requirements and meeting them). He doesn't call it 'strategy', he calls it 'common business sense'.

When my son was less than two years old, he embarked on a strategy aimed at acquiring a cuddly rabbit made by one of his elder sisters at a 'build-a-bear' workshop. It took him over six months of persistent strategic implementation – but it was successful.

If you and I, someone without qualifications and a young child can formulate and implement strategies effectively, the myth is disproven – strategy is not only for the hyper-intelligent!

Strategy is not only for the top board

In *Strategies of the Serengeti* I call this 'the elephants mating myth' – the myth suggests that strategy is something that is done at very high level, with a lot of grunting and groaning and takes about two years to see any measurable results.

Far too often in business, we have middle management paralysis. They choose not to take action as they are waiting for direction and wisdom from the board. Seldom does this waiting produce the strategic direction they crave. Good management teams readily communicate sufficient vision and direction to inspire and enable the middle management to make decisions and take action. Poor management teams do not communicate and get what they deserve – middle management is afraid to take action in case it is not in accordance with the strategy they think the senior executives must be working on, but seldom are.

Strategy formulation is for all levels of the business – we each create the strategy pertinent to our role and level. For some it may be the direction of the whole company, for a retail store manager it may be about where to site the best-selling products and how to allocate shelf space to the entire range. Either and both are strategy. Strategy is for all.

Strategy is not a big document

The annual strategic planning process of some organizations is a time-consuming exercise on filling in analyses, completing a SWOT[1], compiling compelling narrative and is accomplished with the use of more human resource than it would take to manage a small nation. The result, after copious revisions, is a cumbersome document. This is not strategy, it is the production of a work of narrative fiction of questionable use.

Strategy is not an annual exercise, it is an ongoing evolving discipline. It constantly changes in response to initiatives and changes in the market and the business. Earlier today, I was talking with a senior clinician in the British National Health Service. He had generated an idea and sought to implement it but was told that he cannot have the resources for it, regardless of the almost immediate benefit it would yield because 'it is not in your strategic plan'. The advice was to put it into next year's strategic plan and when that was signed off by the executive, he could enact it. This would be a delay of many months and would see many months' benefit foregone – madness. In this case the strategic plan has become a limiter, an inhibitor and a barrier to initiative and progress.

In MBAs, all students are taught about 'emergent strategies' (opportunities and the ability to take advantage of them), which were unforeseen. Innovative, fast-moving companies are much better at taking such advantages than those encumbered by a concrete business plan. They are also taught about 'unrealized strategies', which were pertinent at the time the strategic plan was developed, but became redundant between that time and the present. For example, the 2008 global banking crisis suddenly threw the market into turmoil. All banks' expansive and acquisitive strategies became instantly unrealizable and the immediate implementation of survival strategies became paramount. By 2009, none were following their beautifully created strategic plans of 2008.

It is worth completing a strategic plan, on the condition that it is as an ongoing exercise and takes no more than a few days to compile, as it sets direction and seeks to draw together disparate activities. However, a strategic plan as an inhibitive cumbersome document is not strategy, it is bureaucracy.

Strategy is and is not like a journey

The journey analogy has significant merit but it also has limitations. Following the journey template below will add value to your strategic planning and is worth doing.

Journey template

- *Where am I? – a realistic assessment of your current position*
- *Where do I want to get to? – your intended business destination*
- *What are my options for getting there?*
- *What are the various bases on which I make that choice? – for example, is time critical? Is there a geographical remit or limitation?*
- *For those options, what resources will I need?*
- *Once a choice is made, what are my staging posts? – where should I be in 6 months? 1 year? 2 years?*
- *Do I have agreement and buy-in from all relevant stakeholders?*

Now start the journey.

- *Check – am I on track? Am I meeting my staging posts? Is this destination still my destination?*

This is a good and valuable exercise, which I recommend. However, the journey analogy has disadvantages in that, like all analogies, it can break down. To perpetuate the analogy, if my journey was from New York (present location) to San Francisco (intended destination), I could have options of fly or drive. Perhaps I will choose to drive and acquire the relevant resources – car, credit card, map and so on. I then start the journey. I keep on track and am meeting my staging posts.

In this simple example, San Francisco will always be west. I will not wake up one morning and find that plate tectonics has moved San Francisco into Canada. I will not wake up one morning and find that roads no longer exist and so the motor vehicle in which I am travelling is now redundant technology and requires immediate replacement. However, in business, such factors can occur. The destination can change rapidly, indeed instantaneously. The route to market or mode of travel can change equally rapidly and good strategy is able to encompass this.

An example of such change could be the impact on US company Hoover when UK entrepreneur James Dyson developed the bagless vacuum cleaner. Both the 'destination' and the 'mode' to get there changed for Hoover – the old way of doing things was no longer appropriate. Hoover was previously able to sell the vacuum cleaning machines at a low margin as it would make a large profit on the repeat purchase consumables of the vacuum cleaner bag. Dyson changed the market in one stroke. Hoover could no longer rely on a strategy of large profits and ever increasing sales from the old technology and had to readjust strategy. The lost opportunity that Hoover had to eliminate this threat will be discussed later.

So, do use the journey analogy when formulating strategy, but do also bear in mind that the route and destination is for constant consideration and may change in response to external or internal factors at any time.

Having established what strategy is not...

- military
- only for the hyper-intelligent
- only for the top board
- a big document
- totally like a journey

...let us now consider what strategy is. This is not easy as different people use the word to mean different things. If you are given the task to 'become more strategic' in your Personal Development Plan, it is quite difficult to make that SMART (Specific, Measurable, Achievable, Relevant, Timely), which is always a good challenge to those who have requested that objective for you! Part of the reason for this is the variety of uses of the term and the nebulous nature of several of these uses.

Strategy Safari by Henry Mintzberg *et al.* is a superlative journey through the various aspects of academic strategy and in my opinion should definitely be read by students as part of an academic study of strategy. However, for the non-academic, he adds, in Chapter 1, a summary of his five Ps of strategy based on a 1987 article[2]. I will replicate his five Ps with my own interpretation and examples.

Strategy is a plan

As such, strategy is an intended course of action that steers an organization to achieve what it has set out to achieve. It is a plan that gives us a destination, or vision – it demonstrates an intended direction and it gives us guidance on where to go and where not to go.

However, few of us ever do exactly as we planned – the market is constantly changing and the strategy adapts accordingly. Sometimes, things just do not go as planned or sometimes we make decisions that are not part of the plan.

Strategy as a plan is fine – but the plan is an intended route from which there may be considerable variation. When Nokia was felling trees, it had no plan to move into telecommunications – the plan evolved on a step-by-step basis.

Strategy is a plan, but a constantly evolving plan.

Strategy is a pattern of behaviour

The second 'P' is that of strategy as a series of behaviours that form a pattern. The organization generates a consistency of behaviour that becomes its strategy. In the vehicle industry, the Italian company Ferrari produces some of the greatest works of motorized technology on the planet. A Ferrari is all about aspiration, expensive, fast, sporty. The pattern of behaviour of this brand and company has generated an icon. If I were to suggest a budget-priced, small-engined Ferrari family car or estate (US: station wagon), you would correctly laugh – it does not fit the pattern of behaviour and so would be a wholly inappropriate choice.

Conversely, involvement in the world Formula 1 championship fits exactly into the behavioural pattern of the brand and company – which is why they do it.

Volkswagen is a highly successful German vehicle manufacturer. They have a range of brands encompassing different areas in the market:

High: Bugatti, Lambourgini, Bentley
Medium to high: Audi
Medium: Volkswagen
Medium to low: Skoda, Seat (Seat is making a market
                   change to become a more sporty offering
                   but emerged from this low end of the
                   market.)

However, the introduction of the luxurious, technically superior, beautifully crafted Volkswagen Phaeton defied all of their carefully arranged multi-brand strategy. A US$ 100,000+ vehicle with a VW badge on it does not fit the pattern. VW equals mid-market; US$ 100,000+ is higher end of the market. The Phaeton did not fit with the pattern and was rightly rejected by the car-buying public. VW were manufacturing at less than 20 per cent of the capacity for this unwanted non-pattern product. It exhibited a wrong strategy by not understanding that strategy is a pattern of behaviour.

Strategy is a position in the market

My perception of the differences between the 'pattern' and the 'position' is that 'pattern' is the behaviour you choose – it is internal to the business and within your control. I perceive 'position' as an external, market-related aspect of strategy – where you are in your chosen markets. Here, you are less in control, with the potential to be buffeted by the waves of the competitive activity and the ever-shifting winds of the customer's desires.

What position in the market will you choose and why? Some companies choose to sell a product as cheaply as possible, aspiring to gain profitability through high volume, while another will choose to sell a smaller volume of more expensive premium-priced products. I may pay £5 for a bottle of the French wine Cahors, but I may pay £50 for a Champagne. The companies producing both have strategies to be profitable, the former having to sell many more bottles than the Champagnery. Some companies will choose to position themselves in a distinct niche, some will position themselves as a mass-market provider. Coca-Cola is the world's number one brand and number one carbonated drink. However, in Scotland it is number two. IrnBru rules the geographical niche of Scotland. IrnBru has chosen a position of geographical niche that has proven sustainable over decades despite every effort by the global number one to become the Scottish number one.

Strategy is a perspective

Mintzberg uses the P of perspective to mean the organization's way of doing things in a similar way to how Marvin Bower defined culture as 'the way we do things around here'[3]. I would prefer to use his own example of the Egg McMuffin but in a slightly different way.

The Egg McMuffin argument 1:
It is merely a minor product extension. McDonald's have taken their standard burger product, softened the bun slightly, extracted the burger and relish, substituting it with bacon and egg. The Egg McMuffin is a product change – a variety from an existing product.

The Egg McMuffin argument 2:
It is a wholescale change of approach in the market. Previously, McDonald's burgers were a 11 a.m. to 11 p.m. offering. The McMuffin has allowed the business to create a breakfast market offering a new eating occasion to their menu and a new opportunity to buy at McDonald's for its customers. McDonald's can now serve the public, and make money, from 6 a.m until 11 p.m.

Whichever perspective you take will impact your strategic decision-making. If VW had the perspective that the VW brand is mid-range, they would not have launched the Phaeton. If Mercedes-Benz had the perspective that they were executive saloon specialists, they would probably still dominate that market. If McDonald's had the perspective that they were a burger chain, they would not have created a breakfast market.

Strategy is a ploy

Others will use the word 'strategy' to mean a 'ploy' or a specific action aimed at outmanoeuvring a competitor. One of my favourite ploys was Marlboro day, 2 April 1993, when cigarette manufacturer Philip Morris cut the price of their branded cigarettes in the US by 20 per cent in response to ongoing erosion of their sales by lower price alternatives. The price of Marlboro's stock fell by 26 per cent (approx US$ 10 billion) and other branded companies suffered stock falls as 'the death of the brand' was heralded. This, however, was a myopic western-centric focus. It was also a ploy. Competitor J. R. Reynolds had little option but to copy the strategy or lose ground. They therefore also suffered loss of cash, profitability and stock price. Once Philip Morris estimated that J. R. Reynolds were sufficiently cash-weakened to be unable to respond, they launched a marketing campaign in Russia and Eastern Europe, which resulted in Marlboro being a highly sought after, profitable and successful brand there. It was at the very top of that market for well over a decade until Japanese Tobacco managed to topple it – a great ploy in the US to gain success in the higher growth Eastern European market.

The Western press focussed almost exclusively on the effects in the US and ignored the wider global successes, which were longlasting and highly profitable. Even in the US, Marlboro regained its lost stock price within two years and history has shown it to be a ploy that generated success sustained for a considerable time.

Summary

Understanding what strategy is and what it isn't is not easy because so many people have different opinions on the matter and use different definitions. Many also perpetuate myths that are unhelpful to understanding strategy. In this chapter, we have shown that strategy is not:

- military
- only for the hyper-intelligent
- only for the top board
- a big document.

We have also shown that strategy can be considered to be like a journey but that the analogy, like all analogies, breaks down. Strategic destination, intention and route can change more dramatically than seismic transformation can change a landscape.

We have shown that strategy can equally be some or all of the five Ps:

- plan – an intended set of actions
- pattern – a consistent behaviour
- position – a location of products in a market
- perspective – a view, opinion or stance
- ploy – a manoeuvre

SUNDAY

MONDAY

TUESDAY

WEDNESDAY

THURSDAY

FRIDAY

SATURDAY

The intention of strategy is to give direction, boundaries and co-ordination of effort to seek to achieve our objectives for our organization. Without this, the organization will almost certainly fail.

'There are two types of business: those who have their strategy right and those who are going out of business.'
Stephen Berry

Questions (answers at the back)

1. What is the definition of the word strategy?
   a) Planning a journey ❑
   b) Creating activity ❑
   c) Achieving results ❑
   d) Leading an army ❑

2. Why is the military analogy inadequate? (note – 2 correct answers)
   a) The terminology is inappropriate in business ❑
   b) The chain of command is different in business and the military ❑
   c) It assumes an endpoint of victory when business has no end point ❑
   d) Military focus is on the enemy, strategy on the customer ❑

3. What are the dangers of a strategic plan document?
   a) It may get lost ❑
   b) It can become too static and inflexible ❑
   c) It is not seen by everyone in the company ❑
   d) It can be used to prop open fire exits ❑

4. What are the advantages of using the 'journey' analogy for strategy?
   a) It is easy to understand and communicate ❑
   b) It creates a solid unchanging plan ❑
   c) Many people use it ❑
   d) It may identify hidden resources ❑

5. What is the first step in using the journey analogy for strategy?
   a) Analysis of where we are ❑
   b) Analysis of where we want to get to ❑
   c) Consideration of obstacles on the route ❑
   d) Understand why we want to make the journey ❑

6. Why would a low-cost Ferrari family car be a bad idea?
   a) The price would be wrong ❑
   b) It does not fit the pattern of behaviour that has made the brand successful ❑
   c) As a ploy, it would be too radical ❑
   d) Americans prefer American cars ❑

7. Why have Volkswagen not manufactured the Phaeton at maximum capacity?
   a) It is a high-tech, superior vehicle and the complexities of the computer systems mean that it takes longer to manufacture ❑
   b) It has not been adequately marketed as all its attributes have not been advertised sufficiently ❑
   c) It is a high-prestige car with a medium-market badge – and does not fit the pattern of behaviour of the VW marquee and so the public have rejected it ❑
   d) As it is new technology, it is prone to breaking down ❑

MONDAY

Understand what drives strategy and what strategy drives

The purpose of strategy is to take an organization from where it is to where it wants to be. As such, strategy does not exist alone, in isolation from all other aspects of the business; it is integral to everything within the business. Most organizations have the following:

- vision
- strategic plan
- budget
- culture
- structure
- brand
- public relations message
- corporate and social responsibility.

However, these are frequently disparate and unconnected. For example, the organizational structure is not about getting people's names and roles in boxes, then connecting them with lines and dotted lines. The organizational structure is not about communication, nor about reporting. Its primary purpose is to facilitate the effective implementation of the organizational strategy. If it is not doing that, it is the wrong structure. There is nothing new in that argument – Alfred Chandler stated it in 1962 – but many organizations have not listened. Many see the aspects above as distinct and not inter-related.

This chapter will show where strategy fits into the business, what drives strategy and what strategy affects. As a bonus, it will also contextualize the other factors above – where they fit into business.

Organizational vision

The primary driver of any organization is its vision. This is what it seeks to achieve – its purpose on this planet.

> *'Good business leaders create a vision, articulate the vision, passionately own the vision, and relentlessly drive it to completion.'*
>
> Jack Welch

> *'The very essence of leadership is that you have to have a vision.'*
>
> Theodore Hesburgh

> *'We think too small, like the frog at the bottom of the well. He thinks the sky is only as big as the top of the well. If he surfaced, he would have an entirely different view.'*
>
> Mao Tse-Tung

All other aspects of the business must be driven by this vision as they are the means by which the vision becomes a reality – and this includes the organizational strategy.

In many cases, so called 'vision statements' are mere words on paper – they are not visions. For a vision to be a vision, it must achieve certain tasks:

- Drive and direct the business
- Inspire and motivate the staff
- Determine and set the goals
- Initiate and steer the strategy
- Establish and challenge the ethics, values, modus operandi – 'the way we do things around here' (Bower)

Vision impacts everything. If it doesn't, it's not a vision.

Some authors and consultants try to make different definitions of vision, mission, or purpose. I don't support such semantics and have never seen such a discussion add any value. I am happy to use those words interchangeably but prefer 'vision'. Most importantly, its job is to propel everything which the organization and the people in it seek to do.

The most important people in the success or impotence of a vision are the organizational top team. If they merely pay lip service to a theoretical set of words, the 'vision statement' simply isn't a vision for the organization. If, however, they are the most passionate drivers of the vision and 'live' the vision stronger, more consistently and more fervently than anyone else, both they and the vision are doing their jobs.

How does the vision drive strategy?

The vision states the intention. This will drive a series of goals. I have seen these goals in many formats for many companies, but for the vast majority they seem to be the same five – a goal each on:

- what we do
- how we do it
- our customers
- our people
- money.

Some readers will now be wondering why they have just paid hundreds of thousands of dollars to a consultancy to help develop their goals – and yet they still have these five!

SUNDAY
MONDAY
TUESDAY
WEDNESDAY
THURSDAY
FRIDAY
SATURDAY

The purpose of the goals is to set out what needs to be achieved in order to make the vision a reality. Some writers use the word 'objectives' for these goals. I choose not to as 'objectives' are frequently used in personal performance management where the objectives are SMART. The 'goals' we are now discussing do not necessarily have to be SMART. They can be so – this is not a prohibitive statement, it is just not a necessary requirement. For example, if the goal is 'to have the best, the most innovative and the most satisfied staff in the industry', it is an ongoing goal – the T of 'timely' is missing. These high-level goals, driven by the organizational vision, are not intended to be changed frequently. They should have equal longevity with the vision. Conversely, the 'objectives' of Personal Development Plans should be achieved and developed as progress in the plan proceeds. The 'goals' do not change very often, if at all; the 'objectives' can change as fast as you can achieve them.

These goals then drive the strategy. The strategy comprises the things that the business is doing in order to achieve the goals in order to make the vision a reality. Whether the 'things' are the strategy of plan, pattern, position, perspective or ploy, their task is to achieve the goals so that the vision is accomplished.

To continue our goal example of 'to have the best, the most innovative and the most satisfied staff in the industry', we would put in place strategies to achieve this goal. These would include:

- A remuneration strategy – you will not get the best people in the industry without a top quartile pay policy.
- A recruitment strategy – people are not a blank canvas – they come with experience and preconceptions. If the goal involves the best, the most innovative and the most satisfied, the recruitment strategy needs to target those who show the attributes required and therefore are more likely to be satisfied in your business. You would not recruit a conservative, risk-averse person to a company that prizes innovation – the company will not achieve its goals and the person will be dissatisfied and stressed.

- An engagement strategy – actions to ensure that the staff are emotionally engaged with the business and its vision. It is a truism that a person's physical presence at a place of work can be bought, but their emotional engagement has to be earned, coaxed and nurtured.
- A leadership strategy – the adage that people tend not to leave companies, they leave bosses, inevitably has an element of truth in it. If our goal includes 'satisfied staff', we need to have a strategy of generating the best business leaders we can.

There are many more staff related strategies, but for brevity I will pause there and ask you to derive another five or six areas of strategy to achieve this goal. Perhaps you may choose to look at:

- location strategies – office location and amount of home working
- premises – don't expect creativity in a sterile office
- performance management process – the outputs of a good 'PM' process are direction, development and motivation
- bonus, reward and recognition system
- technology
- staff learning, training and development
- organizational communication
- and many more.

There is nothing new in this progression of Vision – Goal – Strategy. I have seen a variety of versions, for example MOST (mission – objective – strategy – tactics), POST (purpose – objectives – strategy – tactics), VAST (vision – aims – strategy – tactics), PAST and so on. They all seek to do the same thing: to drive the vision into reality by creating goals (or objectives or aims), then generating the strategies to achieve the goals and then going further to let the strategy drive the shorter-term tactics, which then, when accumulated, realize the strategic intent (i.e. achieve what you set out to achieve).

Sometimes I observe conversations seeking to differentiate between strategy and tactics. Again, as with vision, mission and purpose, I would term these discussions non-value-adding semantics and have never seen them yield any benefit to a business. One person's tactics can be another person's strategy depending on their role and position within the business. I would advise progressing through to practical action rather than debating about which box something should sit in.

The ladder of business success

However, I would argue that stopping at 'tactics' is one step short. I would also argue that this progression does not adequately engage or position the elements such as brand, culture and structure that we mentioned at the beginning of this chapter. To alleviate these omissions, I use a 'ladder'. With the ladder analogy, we start climbing at the bottom rung and move upwards. Each rung is important and if one is missing the ladder becomes dangerous and has the potential of not achieving its purpose (in our case, business success). It should also be noted that, for a ladder to function correctly, each rung should be firmly connected to the uprights on each side and also that the uprights are parallel – that is, they are both going in the same direction.

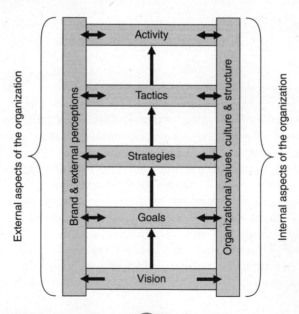

The rungs

The progression from vision to tactics has been discussed. However, by adding the fifth rung, activity, I am seeking to ensure that what we do on a day-to-day basis is firmly driven by the organizational vision and hence each little activity from each individual is taking us one step closer to making the tactics succeed, which combined result in a successful strategy, which collated mean achieved goals, which then result in a realized vision.

For example, the UK retailer John Lewis has achieved a great progression from vision to activity in the rare instances when the customer is dissatisfied and seeks to return a product. The vision is about success in its areas of activity as a high street retailer; the goals include aspects of customer satisfaction. It is easy to have satisfied customers when everything is going well and there are many strategies John Lewis instigates to enhance this. However, it takes genuine class to have exemplary customer satisfaction when things have gone badly. John Lewis therefore has strategies to enhance customer satisfaction that relate to the times when dissatisfaction is encountered. This percolates into tactics that include how they train their staff to deal with customers, their process for handling problems and, the one I want to focus on, for when the customer wishes to return a product.

So far we have a clear link between the vision and the tactics of dealing with returned goods. But what if I went into a store with a product to return, probably stressed by the situation, and then had an argument with a member of staff exhibiting poor attitude and no desire to assist the customer? The faulty product, my own stress and the poor attitude of the staff all compound to give me a wholly dissatisfied scenario and I may decide never to shop at that store again. The strategy is clear – strategies to ensure satisfied customers. The tactics are clear – an array of tactics to deal with returned goods. However, in this example the whole compilation of vision up to tactics would collapse if the activity was wrong – the staff member was unhelpful and did not enact the tactics, or strategy or goals, and negatively impacted on the vision.

SUNDAY MONDAY TUESDAY WEDNESDAY THURSDAY FRIDAY SATURDAY

In many retail stores worldwide, that is the experience customers have when returning faulty goods. Not in John Lewis. In John Lewis, a customer enters the store to return a product. The place to go is clearly marked. The staff are well trained, polite, helpful and utterly professional in ensuring that the customer walks out of the store with a superlative customer experience, a new, working product (if that is what they want) with no problem, no argument and more importantly, with an attitude that means they will return to John Lewis to shop again.

Anyone can provide good customer service for satisfied customers. Few manage it for dissatisfied customers. I use the John Lewis example of this connectedness of the ladder when speaking at business conferences in the UK. So far dozens of people in the audiences will willingly extol the virtues of John Lewis from their experience of when things have gone wrong and they return a product. I ask them to give John Lewis a score out of 10 for their customer experience when in such a stressed and negative scenario. Most give 10. Many give 9. But I've only heard two people give low scores of 4 and 5, and in fairness, I think the 4 contributed to her own misfortune!

A more international example in the retail sector is that of the Apple shops. The vision, and everything about the company, is about innovation, superior technology, cutting edge design, passion for the brand and high fashion electrical products. By simply walking into a store you observe activities that illustrate all of these. The rungs are fully connected and the strategies are in their rightful place – driving the tactics and daily activities in order to achieve the goals in order to make the vision a reality.

The left upright

This represents all external factors of the business – the brand and the perception of the company by all outside of it: customers, potential customers, suppliers, shareholders, the public, governments.

If this left upright exists separate from the rest of the business, the ladder in our analogy would collapse. The vision drives the goals and in due course the strategy, tactics and activities but it also drives the left upright. The business, driven by the vision, uses strategies, tactics and activities to impact and influence everything on the left upright. This is where brand strategy, advertising tactics, and public relations activity interface. They do not exist on their own, they are part of the ladder of business success seeking to make the vision a reality. If a brand strategy is in conflict with the vision, it is a wrong brand strategy. Using the example of Mercedes-Benz from the introduction, I do not know what the vision, goals and strategies were or are, but I can observe that either the vision had no desire to continue the enviable, premium, aspirational positioning the business held in the vehicle market, or, if it did, the brand strategy of putting the same brand to a series of small cars was in utter conflict with it.

The strategies of corporate and social responsibility exist here. Their purpose is to present the company in the best manner for achieving the perception it requires, ultimately to assist in achieving the vision. Toy manufacturer Hasbro has built a children's hospital in Rhode Island, US. It is a monumental and wholly admirable commitment to children. It is also a huge physical barrier to any criticism of the commercial and profitable New York stock exchange listed company as it seeks to market its products to children. This is a corporate and social responsibility strategy seeking to enable the business vision. Virgin Atlantic Airline collects passengers' spare currency and channels it, as many other airlines do, into doing good in developing world communities. The in-flight video shows VAA crew, in their uniforms, interacting with children in sub-Saharan Africa. It is part of a very convincing public relations strategy, about which the staff seem genuinely engaged. Does it help achieve the vision? Absolutely! Having seen the video in-flight, it adds positive impressions about the company, brand and staff in my mind – so I am more likely to return as a customer.

The right upright

This represents all the factors that are internal to the company and therefore within its control. Some of them are easier than others to control – structure is relatively simple to construct, culture is infinitely more complex – but they are still internal factors that the company can influence at will.

The purpose of strategy is to make the vision become a reality (via achieving the goals). The purpose of structure is to facilitate the success of the strategies, tactics and activities, which in due course (via strategies and goals) seek to make the vision a reality. The purposes of culture or values or organizational processes are all the same – to achieve the vision. In many cases, this connection does not seem to be realized; the link of rung to upright is then broken and the ladder is unsafe.

Strategy (and tactics and activity) interface with all these elements. We can have a strategy of cultural change – to help achieve the vision. We can have a strategy of embedding our company values – to help achieve the vision.

Failure to make these vital connections, either between the progression of the rungs as we climb the ladder or between rungs and either of the uprights, generates an unsafe ladder. This leads to poor co-ordination of business activity, lack of direction and purpose, uncertainty and is ultimately a sign of poor leadership as it is one of the core responsibilities of the top executives to make their vision a reality. Failure to make these connections means that an organization runs the risk of being dragged in one direction by its budget, another direction by its brand, a third by its values, another by its culture and yet another by its vision. Any business being dragged in so many directions by such varied competing factors is doomed.

Summary

Strategy, or any other facet of business such as culture, brand, recruitment, structure or public relations, should not exist in a separate bubble with the organization appearing as an amalgam of a vast number of these unrelated bubbles. The organizational vision drives everything – including strategy. The vision is the statement of desire – what or where the business wants to be. This will require the achievement of a number of goals. The job of strategy is to find a way or route to achieve these goals. This way or route is then broken down into lower-level, shorter-term chunks termed 'tactics', which in turn are translated into the day-to-day activity of every employee. Each person is therefore making small contributions to the achievement of the vision with each action.

All strategies fit here – driven by vision and driving action – whether they are brand strategies, advertising strategies, human resources strategies, whole-company strategies, product strategies or any other of the myriad of possible strategies that a business will embark on as it seeks to turn its vision aspiration into a reality.

SUNDAY
MONDAY
TUESDAY
WEDNESDAY
THURSDAY
FRIDAY
SATURDAY

Questions (answers at the back)

1. What drives everything in a business?
a) The vision ❏
b) The strategy ❏
c) The Chief Executive ❏
d) The customer ❏

2. Why do some 'vision statements' not actually fulfil the function of a vision?
a) They are not adventurous enough ❏
b) The staff cannot recite them ❏
c) They do not direct and inspire the people ❏
d) The customer doesn't understand them ❏

3. What did Theodore Hesburgh say about vision?
a) Organizations should have one ❏
b) They must be well communicated ❏
c) A lack of vision will give a lack of direction ❏
d) Vision is the very essence of leadership ❏

4. Which of these is NOT a requirement of a vision?
a) To determine and set the goals ❏
b) To initiate and steer the strategy ❏
c) To establish and challenge the ethics ❏
d) To communicate the business to the customers ❏

5. Why does the ladder model use the term 'goals' rather than 'objectives'?
a) To ensure a differentiation between these and performance management objectives ❏
b) Because they are aims rather than achievable targets ❏
c) Because they do not have to be SMART ❏
d) Because the author prefers football terminology ❏

6. What is the purpose of an organization's structure?
a) To show where people fit into the business ❏
b) To help the successful implementation of the strategy ❏
c) To demonstrate who reports to whom ❏
d) To give staff career aspirations ❏

7. What is the purpose of an organization's culture?
a) To keep staff motivated ❏
b) To make the workplace an enjoyable place to be ❏
c) To help the successful implementation of the strategy ❏
d) To give the Human Resources department something to talk about ❏

8. Why should strategy, vision, culture, brand, budget and so on be integrated?
a) It makes them easier to manage ❑
b) Lack of integration pulls the company in many different directions ❑
c) It looks better for shareholders ❑
d) It saves duplication of effort ❑

9. What is an organization's vision?
a) A statement of what it sees as its purpose and what it seeks to achieve ❑
b) A statement that will inspire the employees to greater achievement ❑
c) A statement to draw all aspects of the business together ❑
d) A statement of how the business sees itself in the marketplace ❑

10. Who are the most important influences on whether the vision succeeds or fails?
a) The employees ❑
b) The customers ❑
c) The top team/board ❑
d) The Human Resources department ❑

TUESDAY

Understand internal strategy

Strategy can apply to the direction taken by the entire business; for example, whether it focusses on a small niche market such as Scottish beverage IrnBru or a ubiquitous global market such as Coca-Cola; whether it focusses on selling large numbers of low-margin products or a smaller number of higher-margin products, such as the budget airlines or the executive-focussed global carriers; whether it seeks to innovate, like Gillette, or follow the leader as Wilkinson Sword does; whether it progresses one idea at a time in the market, as Apple usually does, or multiple ideas unsure of which will succeed, as drug companies do. However, these sort of strategic decisions are likely to be beyond the reach of most readers. For most people, their first encounter with business strategy is in implementing some form of internal strategy. It is still strategy – any of the five Ps – it is still driven by the organizational vision, and is still vital in moving towards achieving the company goals.

This chapter will explore some of the areas within any business where we need success. Each of them is critical and a failure in any one can generate an inability to achieve what the company has set out to do. The chapter will focus on the internal building blocks of business and the strategies to get them right.

The building blocks of business

There are a number of key areas in business that are critical for success. We need to ensure that we have strategies in place to generate a desired outcome for each of them. The 'building blocks of business' model identifies seven areas and aims, to impress on any business the importance of strategies to manage and maximise the benefit of each of them while also identifying potential vulnerabilities and then generating internal strategies to remove these vulnerabilities.

The model can also be used at department or team level, so the aspiring manager can use this structure early in their career.

The seven building blocks are:

Strategy	
Finance	Processes
People	Technology
Product	Marketing

Most of us will have taken examinations at some point in our lives. In almost all exams, a score of six out of seven would have generated a healthy pass (over 85 per cent!). However, in this structure six out of seven is not good enough. Six out of seven will leave one vulnerable area through which failure can flow into the company, division or team. The overall internal strategy – part of the right upright of the ladder of business success – is to derive strategies for developing each of the seven areas. We will consider some aspects of each of the seven, but first pose a question: *Where is the customer?*

The seven building blocks do not include the customer, yet we have established that the aim of business is to profitably satisfy customer needs. Surely this model cannot be suggesting that we ignore the customer in strategy formulation?

Indeed, it isn't. The customer has to be paramount in each of the blocks, not a separate block on its own. Unless each block is customer focussed, it is unlikely to be performing its role effectively.

Throughout this chapter I will give some examples of relevant strategy from well-known companies but also some from my own experience and career. All my career examples are true but the companies remain anonymous to protect my former work colleagues!

Product

Product strategies are about producing what people will buy. Traditionally we have expressed such strategy as meeting a customer need, but as Apple have shown with the iPhone and iPad, they can create the need – the customer didn't know they needed an iPad until the late Steve Jobs told them that they did!

Progressing this, the 'need', is equally valid whether it is a real need or a perceived need. In Japan, it is common practice to wear a facemask to prevent the transmission or receiving of cold or flu germs from other people. The germs are airbourne and so are able to pass freely through the mask, which has little practical purpose. However, the need is perceived and millions are sold to Japanese citizens worldwide. Similarly in the Western world, millions of dollars, pounds and euros are spent on vitamins, supplements and herbal concoctions with no discernible scientific advantage – but the advantage is perceived and profits made as a result.

Conversely, I sometimes hear of businesses complaining that their product is extremely useful for meeting a customer need, but the customer does not seem to realize it. If the customer does not realize it, the need is not perceived, so there is no use for the product until the customer does realize it. To get a 'tick' in this product box, the product must meet a clearly defined need and the customer must be fully in agreement that it does so. The organization needs to have in place product strategies to enhance this. These would include new product development strategies.

Further aspects of product strategy will be discussed in the next three chapters on marketing, brand and competitive strategies. We will therefore save exploration of considering 'product' until then. For today's chapter, we will just acknowledge that a product meets a need of a customer – a real or a perceived need.

People

We have already covered some examples of people strategies in yesterday's chapter (remuneration, recruitment, engagement, leadership, working environment, performance management, bonus reward and recognition). We will therefore be brief in the examples in this section.

I worked briefly in one business where the strategy was to pay the manufacturing staff the lowest pay possible. I also worked in a company where the remuneration strategy was that we would pay the highest in the industry by some considerable amount so that anyone leaving would be paid significantly less for the same job in any rival company.

For both these businesses, I would say that the remuneration strategy was right. For the former, the work was repetitive, functional and did not require significant training, skill or even intelligence. Staff turnover was high as people found better paid jobs, but we were always able to recruit from the ranks of the unemployed. The strategy resulted in keeping costs down and therefore keeping prices to the customer as low as possible. In the second company, the skill requirements were immense. Our reputation was as the premier quality provider in that market and, to my knowledge, we were never the cheapest on any of the tenders we won. Customers were buying a result, not a commodity. Our high pay strategy meant that we were able to choose from the best and the most enthusiastic people in the industry – that strategy enhanced our brand and external perception, and was a strategy wholly in line with achieving our vision of high-quality accomplishments.

Customer-focussed people strategy is about prioritising the effectiveness of those who interface with customers. In one company, we produced the organization organogram with the customer being at the top. The highest employee on the chart was the receptionist – the customer's first point of contact with the company. Customer-focussed people strategy is about training people to give 'John Lewis level' service and rewarding them when they do. The same applies if the customer is an internal customer in your business.

Finance

We have considered having the right product in the market and reviewed some product strategies, but have we got the right product to profitably meet our customer needs? The inclusion of the word 'profitably' is vital as most customers would love to acquire a Rolls Royce car for US$ 1. The customer wins and the company would fail. When car maker British Leyland made the Mini in 1959, they were selling it for £500. It is said that German manufacturer BMW, who ironically now own the Mini brand, looked at the car and concluded that they could not manufacture it for any less than £520 and so concluded that British Leyland must be making a loss on each vehicle. They were. British Leyland had made a simple error of not understanding the building block of finance. They sought to learn from their mistakes. In the 1970s, the nationalized behemoth produced the Hillman Avenger. They worked out how much the car had cost them to make, added a suitable margin and placed the car on the market at £822. The problem was that comparable cars were being sold significantly cheaper – the Ford Escort at £635 and the Vauxhall Viva at £690. They had made another classic mistake of financial strategy – cost plus pricing.

Being successful in this building block is about getting the right product to the right customers at the right price, which means that the customer buys and the company profits. It sounds so simple, but so many mistakes are made. Here are some true examples from my finance career.

Example 1 – flexible plastic manufacture

I worked for a company that made millions of plastic bags for bread, confectionary and snacks, carrier bags and others. Company folklore was that bags made from polypropylene (a type of plastic) generated greater margins than polythene bags. So, when we were behind target on margin, we would ask the sales force to focus on polypropylene. One day I decided to investigate that folklore. It may have been true 15 years earlier when the company was formed, but my investigation showed that polypropylene had a lower margin and therefore when we were short on margin we were instructing the sales force to exacerbate the situation by selling more low-margin product! This would constitute a failure in the finance block of the 'building blocks of business'.

Example 2 – food industry

In another company, we produced a fantastic high quality product, a salmon and broccoli tart. It was an exemplary example of good factory-produced food. However, we found that the customer was only prepared to pay a small premium for this superlative product and if we raised the price higher, demand would fall. We reluctantly took the decision to cease production and use the productive capacity to increase sales of higher-margin, lower-quality and less-exciting quiche Lorraine. Profits from that manufacturing line soared. Producing the product at the price the customer feels is correct is vital for the finance block.

Example 3 – solid plastic manufacture

I had to oversee a manufacturer for a short period of time – it made plastic dustbins and watering cans. Some costs in any environment are fixed – they do not alter with the quantity produced – such as the rent and rates of the factory or office, the office and sales staff salaries, the rental charges on the cars of the sales team. These costs are then spread or proportioned across each product so that the British Leyland Mini error is not replicated. I saw that this company was taking seven seconds to make a waste bin. Competitors were taking three seconds. The company was therefore producing less than half the quantity of product that the competitors could in the same time. This also meant that the amount of overhead apportioned to each waste bin, assuming both companies' costs to be equal, was more than twice that which the competitors apportioned. This company was therefore settling for a lower margin or was pricing their product too high.

Example 4 – hospital

This example raises the issue that the cheapest may not be the best. In two examples, a centralized procurement department made changes to items used by medical surgeons. One was cheaper paper towels on which they dried their washed hands prior to and during operations. The other was cheaper latex gloves, which they used while operating. In both cases, the procurement decision was detrimental. The paper towels were so thin that the surgeons were using four or five every time they washed their hands, compared with two paper towels previously. Use of paper towelling, at the slightly cheaper price, more than doubled and overall costs increased. The new latex gloves were thinner with a lower-quality latex – but cheaper. For many surgeons, the gloves tore when being put on and so were immediately discarded and another pair used. Again, overall usage rocketed, overtaking the cost saving and overall cost went up. Purchasing strategies need to be thought through!

Customer-focussed finance is about providing the product at the right price on the market. Business-focussed finance is about producing the product at the right cost to make a profit. The correct price is always what the customer is willing to pay and so the best pricing strategy is often to work backwards from there:

- How much is the customer willing to pay?
- How much can I manufacture the product for?
- Does the difference between the two give me adequate margin (or profitability)?
- If not, what strategies can I put in place to increase the value in the customer's opinion and what strategies can I put in place to drive down costs?

Processes

This is an often neglected area of strategic focus but can yield great benefit as McDonald's and Amazon have proven. One of the slickest processes I have witnessed is how McDonald's make a burger. In my job, I often train Finance Directors. I sometimes advise them to visit McDonald's to observe the conversion of raw material into finished product, which is then packaged and rapidly sold – converting it into cash. I tell them that every process in their businesses should be that smooth – whether it is your customer's interface with you or whether it is the generation of your management accounts. Better processes decrease cost and so interface with internal finance strategies, lead to less people frustration and so interface with internal people strategies and can have external customer consequences too, as Amazon demonstrate.

Amazon pioneered 'one click technology' to ensure that it is as easy as possible to buy from them. They recommend potential purchases based on your previous purchase history. They will do everything they can to make the sales process as quick and as easy as can be.

The world of behavioural psychometrics (Myers Briggs, DISC, and over 100 others) has not changed significantly since the creation of these tools in the 1920s to 1940s. In most cases we complete a paper-based questionnaire, send it to an expert for analysis and some time later receive their time-intensive deliberations by post. More recently some have moved to online evaluations which, for the higher-quality more useful reports, are then subject to the same expert deliberation and a delay of only a few days before receiving a document. EvaluationStore.com has built itself as the provider of a process that does what coaches and experts take hours to produce in just a few minutes. An online evaluation is completed and before you have made a cup of tea, a full report and analysis has entered your inbox. They haven't changed the evaluation, just the process by which it is done and by which it is delivered to the customer.

> Think about customer-focussed processes – is your business exceptionally easy to deal with or have you erected barriers to contact, barriers that create time delays or barriers that delay the customer receiving the product?

Technology

The critical factor in considering internal technology strategies is the use of the word 'appropriate'. The overarching question is whether your strategies will yield the appropriate level of technology for the business. It is easy to get seduced by a desire for the latest or greatest when it is not required. One UK discount retailer deliberately chooses the cheapest and lowest level of technology they can get away with. This minimizes their expenditure and the pattern of behaviour (internal) fits with the low-cost positioning in the market (external). Conversely, it would be ludicrous for hi-tech Apple stores to adopt that strategy – there would be an internal/external, pattern/position mismatch.

In Europe and the US, where both labour costs and educational levels are high, high technology levels are likely to be more appropriate than in some other parts of the world. One friend was visiting a hospital in a remote area of sub-Saharan Africa. Some high technology had been generously donated by a well-meaning American charity. However, the hospital did not have the expertise to use it. It was inappropriate technology and lay redundant.

A 2011 example of technology being inadequate was the gadget website EBuyer. They saw the last Monday of November as an opportunity to sell a range of products, online, at very heavily discounted prices – mostly £1. Cameras, games, laptops were offered for £1. However, the increased demand for the products sent website use rocketing and EBuyer had horrendously miscalculated the impact on their server capacity – the website crashed, leaving customers unable to buy due to inadequate planning of the technology.

Marketing

Marketing strategies will be considered more fully in Wednesday's chapter, so we will move on.

Strategy

Every board I have ever been on and every board I have ever worked with has, at some point, degenerated to what I term its 'highest level of irrelevance'. The board comprises of Directors, yet, despite our job titles, we often undertake the less strategic tasks of managing. One of the reasons for this is that it is more within our comfort zones – we are more experienced at the roles that have taken us to the board-table than we are at actually functioning as a board. Our challenge is to ensure that the board (or divisional leadership team) exercises its mandate and requirement to operate at strategic level. If we achieve this, we will be exercising our roles more correctly and undertaking those vital tasks such as considering alternative strategies, exploring whether a strategy is working or not, whether strategic aspects are on track or falling behind.

The best way I have found to do this is to implement the CIMA strategic scorecard (Chartered Institute of Management Accountants). A free-of-charge explanatory download can be obtained from their website CIMAglobal.com.

CIMA strategic scorecard™

Strategic position	Strategic options
Strategic implementation	Strategic risk

Most of us have used versions of Kaplan and Norton's 'balanced scorecard', although I rarely ever see one that is truly balanced – they are usually heavily financially biased. This is a good tool for assisting with the operational aspects of the business and as such is a management tool not a board-level tool, where Directors should direct. My suggested way of keeping strategy on the board agenda and ensuring that the conversation is about the right things and at the right level is to have the four aspects of the scorecards as standing items in the board meeting and in the board information pack – of equal, if not greater importance than the financial report.

What the board members discuss in this strategy section will be different each meeting and they will be dependent on the compilers and providers of board information producing a workable, consistent and appropriate set of material for each meeting. Examples of what should be discussed at each point could include:

- **Position:** Here they would consider large-scale external aspects such as the five Ps or small scale internal aspects such as those covered in this chapter.
- **Choice:** The evaluation of options, the basis of choice, parameters and requirements of that choice.
- **Risk:** What could go wrong? Are there risks in the supply chain? Risks to the customer choice with alternatives and substitute goods? What competitor activity is underway or expected? What internal risks (right side of the ladder) are evident?
- **Implementation:** Are we on track? Is a strategy working? Is it within the parameters we agreed and achieving the requirements we set?

In each case, there will be good information available and relevant discussion possible, but also the process of methodically considering strategy like this will highlight where there is an absence of good-quality information. For example, if we are unaware of competitor activity, this should set all board members' neural alarm bells ringing and the information should be sought.

Summary

Are we selling the right product, with the right people, at the right price and cost, by the right process, with the right technology and the right marketing, and is our overall strategy correct? The 'building blocks of business' mode guides us through this strategic thought process. It seeks to develop a business that actively considers all these aspects, and hopefully can in due time answer 'yes' to each of those questions.

In order to get these right, each block has to have the customer as its focus, but each aspect is internal, within our control or influence. As a template for consideration, it therefore provides us with a checklist of important aspects to contemplate in the strategic development of our business. Used critically, it can highlight weak points in our business strategy and provide the focus of how to improve.

Strategy isn't only about external factors and manoeuvring in the marketplace; it is also about getting ourselves in the right shape and the right format to be effective as a business – strategies for success should include strategies to improve and maximise these internal factors as well as the more high-profile and arguably more exciting external strategies.

SUNDAY
MONDAY
TUESDAY
WEDNESDAY
THURSDAY
FRIDAY
SATURDAY

Questions (answers at the back)

1. What are the building blocks of business?
   a) Product, people, finance, strategy, process, technology, marketing ❏
   b) Product, research, customer, advertising, distribution, logistics ❏
   c) Product, price, plan, place, people, promotion, ❏
   d) Plan, pattern, position, perspective, ploy ❏

2. Why is 'customer' not a building block?
   a) Companies should focus on getting their business right – the customer will follow ❏
   b) There are always sufficient customers if the marketing is correct ❏
   c) Too much customer focus decreases profitability ❏
   d) The customer should be at the heart of every block in the model ❏

3. What is needed for success in the product block?
   a) Having a product available to sell ❏
   b) Having a good process of continuing product development ❏
   c) Having a product that the customer realizes meets their need ❏
   d) Having a range of alternative products for the customer to choose from ❏

4. What is the right price to charge?
   a) A price that satisfies the customer's need and makes a profit ❏
   b) A low price to gain market penetration ❏
   c) A price that makes a profit to make the company sustainable ❏
   d) The highest price the customer will pay ❏

5. What are the sections of the CIMA strategic scorecard?
   a) Customer, market, product, marketing ❏
   b) Analysis, option, choice, implementation ❏
   c) Strategic position, options, risk, implementation ❏
   d) Finance, price, cost, profit ❏

6. What would get a 'tick' in the technology block?
   a) Strategies to secure the best available technology ❏
   b) Strategies to implement new technologies quicker ❏
   c) Strategies to ensure that your technology is better than the competitor's technology ❏
   d) Strategies to ensure the most appropriate level of technology ❏

7. What have EvaluationStore.com done to psychometric profiling tests?

a) Changed the process by making it online and instant ❏

b) Changed the product by making it more modern and relevant ❏

c) Changed the marketing by having only an online offering ❏

d) Changed the strategy by merging behavioural and personality evaluation ❏

8. When would the people remuneration strategy be appropriate to pay the lowest possible?

a) When it is manual work, not office or clerical work ❏

b) When the company needs to save money ❏

c) When it is work in a developing country without a full infrastructure ❏

d) When the work is of a low skill level, easy to train and recruit for ❏

9. When would the people remuneration strategy be appropriate to pay the highest in the market?

a) When a country has a high standard of living ❏

b) When the job is highly skilled and the company wants the best employees ❏

c) When it is a fair trade business and the payment to the producer should be enough to live on ❏

d) When there is a labour shortage and companies are competing for employees ❏

10. What was/is wrong with the finance strategy of cost plus pricing?

a) It could have had mistakes in cost calculation ❏

b) It does not contain contingency in case of manufacturing price movements ❏

c) It is purely internally focussed and does not consider what the market will pay ❏

d) It is old fashioned and more modern methods should be used ❏

WEDNESDAY

Understand marketing strategy

The Chartered Institute of Marketing defines marketing as:

> *'The management process responsible for identifying, anticipating and satisfying customer requirements profitably'*

but adds:

> *'In the fast-moving world of business, definitions rarely stay the same.'*

Marketing strategy would then be the set of processes, or the path taken, to turn that definition into a reality for your organization. However, the 'profitability' requirement and 'customer' centrality demonstrates that it is focussed on the commercial sector. Not-for-profit, government and public sector organizations should equally be concerned about marketing. This definition therefore has some omissions. Conversely, many would argue that the definition is too broad – taken literally it encompasses the majority of what a business does – from procurement and manufacturing to logistics and finance.

The American Marketing Association defines marketing as:

> *'The activity, set of institutions, and processes for creating, communicating, delivering, and exchanging offerings that have value for customers, clients, partners, and society at large'*

And an online dictionary defines it as:

> *'The total of activities involved in the transfer of goods from the seller to the consumer'*

The point is, again, that, like strategy, brand, culture and so on, there is no one clear, unambiguous or even widely accepted definition of marketing.

This chapter will explore what marketing and marketing strategy involve, give a funnel template for considering different strategic aims of any marketing activity and pose a few challenges to think about.

What does marketing involve?

When considering marketing strategy, Business Studies students at secondary schools (US: high schools) are usually taught about the 9Ps of marketing. Each 'P' is one aspect of marketing and each is part of the strategic mix aimed at ensuring business success. When developing our marketing strategy, we are seeking to develop a co-ordinated series of activities, using these 9Ps to facilitate the success of our overall organizational strategy. These Ps are not something to be looked at in isolation; they are the tools for the marketing part of our overall business strategy.

- **Product** – ensuring that a product meets a customer's needs and having a system in place to ensure that this is monitored as customers' needs and wants change.
- **Price** – any product or service is only successful if it is sold at a price that the customer finds acceptable. This 'P' is about getting the price right.
- **Place** – the product must be available – at the right place in the right time. Online trading has revolutionized the 'Place' of marketing as 24/7 availability is now the norm through websites.
- **Promotion** – the communication to the market and the messages that the organization is projecting.
- **Physical layout** – how products are presented to the customer, for example in a retail environment. Supermarkets and grocery stores tend to put essentials such as bread and milk towards the rear of the store to ensure that customers have to walk past many other products to obtain them – and then hopefully make a spontaneous additional purchase. Similarly, it is probably impossible to shop at Ikea and only emerge with one item – their use of layout in their stores takes the customer on a room by room journey with multiple purchasing ideas in each room.
- **Processes** – ensuring that the process enhances the customer buying experience, not hinders it. Compare the positive process of Amazon's one-click process to the torturous fight through

copious numeric options and inevitable queuing to bad-taste music on many company helplines.

- **Provision of customer service** – how the positive customer experience is maximised. British retailer John Lewis, from Monday's chapter, exemplifies success here.
- **People** – ensuring that anyone who comes into contact with a customer is exhibiting the desired marketing message. For example, telephone financial services call centres must have staff who are quick, polite and knowledgeable if customers are to trust them with their money.
- **Physical evidence** – seeking to give the customer evidence that the purchase will achieve what the customer required prior to purchase. For example, written testimonials of holiday hotels, exemplary cleanliness in a doctor's surgery.

Art, not a science

One of the problematic aspects of any marketing effort, with any of the 9Ps, is that it will almost certainly not achieve the anticipated result! If we initiate an advertising campaign (part of the P of promotion) aimed to increase sales by 5 per cent during the duration of the campaign, it is a judgement call, using experience and experts, of what to do, how to do it, where to do it and when to do it. There is usually no ability to spend US$ 10 million on a campaign and receive an automatic guaranteed return of US$ 50 million in additional sales. This campaign may achieve nothing, may exceed expectations, may have an impact only for the duration of the campaign or may have no immediate impact but see results in future months. In all of those examples, the campaign did not do what it set out to do – a 5 per cent sales increase for the duration of the campaign.

There are also very limited opportunities to develop a 'scientific or control experiment' – different marketing strategies in different areas to establish which was most effective; or a marketing initiative in one area and not in another to observe the differences. Even when it is possible, it is not guaranteed that the same result would be achieved upon repetition or, if they are different geographic regions, that the results would be the same if what was done in region A was then done in region B and vice versa.

Marketing therefore requires significant acts of judgement and opinion regarding what would be most effective and most appropriate. In many cases, the actual results are significantly different from the expected results. By 2007, the British confectionary manufacturer Cadbury (now part of Kraft, US) had suffered an erosion of customer confidence due, in part, to a contamination scare in 2006 and its associated expensive product recall and fine by the British Food Standards Agency; and also partly due to the production of Easter eggs with traces of nuts but with no warning of this for those with nut allergies – a potentially fatal condition. Cadbury needed to bring itself back to stronger customer awareness and a more positive image. A marketing campaign for its flagship brand, Cadbury Dairy Milk (CDM) with co-ordinated newspaper, billboard, cinema and television elements was launched in the UK in August 2007 featuring a gorilla drumming to Phil Collins' song 'In the air tonight'. No one could have anticipated the level of success. The YouTube version of the advertisement achieved 500,000 views in the first week, over 6 million within three months; the gorilla had 70 groups set up by fans on Facebook; and various parodies of the advert appeared as advertising homage. Sales of CDM increased by 9 per cent (worth approximately £18 million) and research by YouGov showed that 20 per cent more of the UK population viewed CDM positively after the advertisement campaign than before. The campaign was later expanded internationally.

Marketing may not be aimed at increasing sales

A common misconception is that the function of marketing is to increase sales. That can be one very important function of marketing, but not always.

Sometimes a marketing strategy aims not at achieving the aspects such as greater market share or increased sales, but at less tangible aspects or at minimising negative occurrences. The purpose of a specific piece of marketing effort could include reasons and aims such as:

- Maintaining the present position – few could forget brands such as McDonald's or Coca-Cola, but they continue their high advertising to remain where they are – global top ten brands. Gradual erosion of the message in the customer's mind is almost inevitable unless the message is continually reinforced. Business can be like trying to walk up the downward escalator – if you stay still, you will move backwards. Maintenance marketing seeks to prevent this downward movement.
- Minimizing the negative impact – such as that undertaken by Toyota after the tragically fatal consequences of vehicles accelerating unintentionally and beyond the ability of the brakes to halt the car. The *Los Angeles Times* claimed that there were 1,200 such instances (8 November 2009). In January 2010, Toyota initiated a mass recall of approximately 6.5 million cars to solve the problem. Without effective marketing communication, customers may have been reluctant to buy Toyota again. The impact has relegated Toyota to 11th most valuable brand in 2010 and 2011 from its

height of 6th in 2007 and 2008, but the brand is still valued by Interbrand at just under US$ 28 billion (it peaked at US$ 34 billion in 2008).

- Response to competitive action – having scored such success with its gorilla advertisement, Cadbury could not rest. Mars's galaxy chocolate launched a campaign based on targeting women in 'indulgent moments'. Galaxy increased sales by 12 per cent to £80 million and Cadbury had to respond by almost doubling marketing spend on CDM 2007–8.
- Awareness marketing – some marketing is about starting the potential customer on the route to becoming a purchaser. Efforts at increasing the customers' knowledge of the existence of the company, organization or product are the first step on the journey, but funds from purchasing may not flow in until considerably later in the journey.
- To change perception or behaviour – much of the activity in the not-for-profit sector fits here. Governmental advertising on alcohol awareness is not intended to increase alcohol sales!
- Corporate social responsibility – where a company seeks to communicate its activities to raise its profile as a responsible corporate citizen; for example, in 2011 the UK's National Westminster Bank (part of RBS) launched a national television campaign outlining elements of its community action programme – from how staff go into schools to teach finance, to fundraising for charities.

The marketing funnel

Marketing strategies to achieve any of the 9Ps should be thought through – you need to know exactly what they are intending to do. Ill thought through, vaguely defined, un-specifically targeted marketing effort is frequently wasted effort and wasted money. The strategic intent of any marketing initiative is just as vital as the strategic intent in any other area of strategy – precisely what is any aspect of a marketing strategy seeking to achieve? To help explore this, we can use a 'marketing funnel' to segregate various targets for our marketing strategies.

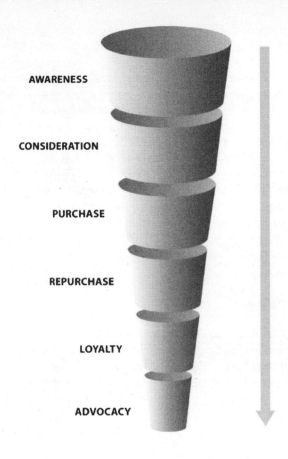

AWARENESS

CONSIDERATION

PURCHASE

REPURCHASE

LOYALTY

ADVOCACY

Awareness

The aim of marketing targeted here is to ensure that those in the group of potential customers who are unaware of the organizational offering become aware of its existence. It is not about sales, but it is the first step towards a sale. Whichever of the 9Ps are used, the message should be consistent with the brand. No one who watches Formula 1 motor racing will fail to notice Ferrari. Few of us move on to the next step of considering purchasing a Ferrari, but the marketing has achieved its objective of alerting us to the existence of the brand.

It is an important point that, in many cases, it is not an automatic aim to progress through the funnel. Traditional, older marketing thinking would seek to drive customers through the funnel and the construction of the diagram hints at a wider audience for awareness, fewer for consideration, even fewer for purchase as some are lost at each stage. Some traditional marketing approaches seek to maximise the speed with which they take customers downwards in the model and minimise the loss of customers at each stage in that movement.

However, not every business and every product wants to drive large quantities of customers all the way through the funnel into the 'advocacy' grouping. In his book *How Brands Grow*, Byron Sharp argues that with a product that

- has a low purchase value
- is a frequent purchase product
- has a wide choice of alternative competing products
- is a rapid or impulsive purchase decision

...a business will create greater business growth from attracting a wide number of customers to buy once than it would from a smaller number of customers buying frequently. Soft drinks, shampoo, beers, wines, many foodstuffs and snacks would be relevant examples.

Consideration

The second sector is marketing activity that is aimed at generating the possibility of purchase in the mind of the potential customer. Not purchase per se, but being conscious of the possibility of purchase. Sometimes the customer movement from 'awareness' to 'purchase' is a huge leap and needs strategies to position the product as a possibility – these are the strategies of 'consideration'. They may take a long time or a short time, but they have a distinct message from the 'buy me' message seeking purchase.

I renew my car every three years and am presently driving a Jaguar. The local Mercedes Benz dealership keeps in telephone contact about every nine months to alert me to news of their products – a marketing strategy aimed at this sector of consideration.

One frequently used tactic in this area is to aim for the product being viewed as having parity with a market leader or with a successful market player. Pepsi has produced some excellent 'anti-coke' advertisements. Coca-Cola outsells Pepsi in all areas of the world excluding the Arabic-speaking world. By attacking the number one, Pepsi seeks to put itself on parity with the number one in the consumer's mind and hence put itself into the category of being considered for purchase as an alternative to the number one.

Purchase

This is marketing effort, any of the Ps, aimed at encouraging the actual buying of the product/service for the first time. It is not unusual for inexperienced marketers to seek to start here without having paid appropriate attention to the previous stages and then wonder why their efforts do not achieve their desires.

Repurchase

These are activities that aim to generate repeat purchase, not necessarily habitual purchase at this phase, just repeat and maybe regular purchase. Budweiser is the best-selling beer in the US and they have spent millions of pounds trying to get firmly established in the British market. Their marketing uses a wide range of the Ps, but they do not appear to generate the repurchase required for firm establishment as a dominant brand. The problem is that we Brits have a different perception from our US cousins of what a beer should taste like. In conferences in the UK, I will sometimes illustrate this point by asking anyone who has ever had a Budweiser to raise their hand. About 90 per cent will normally do so. My follow up question asks those who regularly drink 'Bud' to raise their hands. Never more than 10 per cent raise their hands. My third question is then 'Tell me, where is the problem in Budweiser's strategy?'. The show of hands has made it self-evident. They have great advertising, but it is aimed at the first three stages of the funnel – and has been immensely successful there. They have not, however, aimed anything at the fourth stage – repurchase – and would find that difficult for a European palate.

However, despite almost saturation success at first purchase level, they have continued to pour millions of pounds/dollars into the same hole. Now that Anheuser-Busch is owned by European In-Bev, this futile waste of marketing resource has finished.

Loyalty

Here, we are seeking marketing activity that aims to generate a strong preference of the customer for our product. Marketing strategies in this segment seek to turn repurchase into regular, or habitual, purchase. An example here would be the use of loyalty cards where frequent purchase generates benefits that may or may not apply to the product. My hotel loyalty card enables me to have weekend stays as a benefit while my airline loyalty card allows a wide choice of benefits including the product – free flights – but a vast array of non-flight related goods.

Advocacy

Strategies here seek to develop customer loyalty to the point where they actively recommend the product/service to others and marketing activity here should also facilitate their ability to do so. This is the territory of First Direct Bank – pioneers of telephone and then internet banking. First Direct started a 24/7 telephone banking system on Sunday 1 October 1989. The first 24 hours resulted in 1,000 calls. The concept was simple – banking without branches. Everything could be achieved over the telephone. By 1997, the internet was emerging as a safe and rapidly expanding business vehicle. The extension from telephone banking to internet banking was a natural progression. For each of the last 25 years, polls by MORI and NOP have shown First Direct to be the most recommended bank. A whopping 36 per cent of customers join because they were given personal recommendations – that is the result of existing customers becoming advocates.

Every element of our marketing initiatives should know what it is seeking to achieve and the funnel is an exceptionally useful device to assist us in targeting our marketing strategies and activities.

Above and below the line

You are likely to hear these expressions in discussions about marketing strategies. It will be no surprise to the reader that marketers disagree on exactly what the 'line' is and that they abbreviate the expressions to ATL and BTL. The origins of the terms were from the accounting world when some types of marketing earned the marketing agency a payment of a commission (ATL) and others did not (BTL), but marketing costs have not been charged in this way since about the 1960s, so the reason for the differentiation of two types of marketing expenditure is no longer relevant. However, the terms frequently remain.

My personal preference of definitions is about the line being one of overt visibility and direct customer communication through public media. So ATL would include advertising in newspapers, billboards, radio, cinemas and on televisions. BTL, by my definition, is about things that happen in the background without direct use of public media such as flyers, email marketing, promotions, tensator and end-of-aisle promotions, and sponsorship.

My 'line' of media and direct communication is not a universally accepted definition. Some retain a form of accounting line and others a line that separates mass marketing from niche marketing. However, in real business communication with marketers, my definition is widely understood if somewhat outdated.

A more modern variant is 'through the line' (TTL), which is a sensible co-ordination of both ATL and BTL to be mutually supportive and thus amplify the marketing impact.

Measuring marketing

Marketing spend is an investment for the business and as such requires accountability, control and scrutiny like any other investment. Determining your methods of measurement and what results you are measuring is the key.

Any marketing activity will incur an investment cost. Along with this, you will set:

- distribution targets – proportion of geographical coverage
- rate of sale – for example how many units are sold in a retail store in a week
- repeat purchase rates
- penetration – proportion of the target population who have purchased your product
- redemption rates – for example, how many money-off coupons were used, or for an on-pack promotion (such as a code on a drinks can, input to a site may win the customer £1,000) how many people entered the competition
- sales uplift targets.

The essence of any monitoring of any investment is to establish what you seek to achieve by the investment and then to measure the extent to which you achieved your objectives. Investment in marketing is no different.

... IN THE BEGINNING, NOBODY HAD SET ANY OBJECTIVES, LET ALONE DONE THE COSTING, AND THERE WAS DARKNESS...

There are a myriad of econometric marketing packages available that can strip out different effects such as in-store promotions and pricing to simply identify the effect of the one aspect you are considering – for example, the increased rate of sales due to your advertising campaign rather than the price and promotion effects.

Summary

Marketing has no simple agreed definition, but we have considered it as the 9Ps of getting the right product to the customer in the right way at the right price. An integrated marketing strategy considers all of these Ps and uses them in harmony to achieve the business aspirations. However, marketing strategy and marketing efforts are not exact – they are not a scientific formula where X advertising + Y on-pack promotion = Z sales. Indeed, in many cases marketing activity is not specifically aiming at increasing sales. This often makes justifying it and measuring it difficult.

A useful template for considering marketing strategy is the 'funnel', which demonstrates six distinct aims of a marketing initiative, strategy or campaign. All marketing activity should be able to state precisely what it is aiming to do – whether it is one of the categories not aimed at increasing sales or which of the six elements of the funnel it is seeking to further. Vague marketing aims are likely to be poor strategy and a waste of money. Well thought through, co-ordinated targeted marketing with specific outputs are infinitely more likely to yield success.

Questions (answers at the back)

1. What is the definition of marketing?
   a) Persuading people to buy your product ❑
   b) Presenting your product as an attractive alternative ❑
   c) Selling products, which don't come back, to customers who do ❑
   d) There is no one agreed definition of marketing ❑

2. Which of these are not in the 9Ps?
   a) Provision of customer service ❑
   b) Performance ❑
   c) Physical layout ❑
   d) Provision of evidence ❑

3. What does the P of 'place' refer to?
   a) Making the product available to the customer ❑
   b) Where in the market you choose to sell your product ❑
   c) Whether your sales are online or physical ❑
   d) Which countries you choose to sell your product in ❑

4. Is marketing an art or a science? (Note: two answers)
   a) A science because it can be measured ❑
   b) A science because we have inputs (spend) and outputs (results) ❑
   c) An art because it involves judgement ❑
   d) An art because the results are not able to be predicted specifically ❑

5. Which of the following is NOT a reason to undertake marketing activity that will NOT increase sales?
   a) To keep position in response to a competitor marketing campaign ❑
   b) To spend to minimise the negative impact of a problem ❑
   c) To ensure that the marketing budget is fully spent ❑
   d) To initiate a campaign aimed at making potential customers aware that the product exists ❑

6. Which of the following would NOT be likely to be a marketing strategy aimed at 'awareness'?
   a) Sports sponsorship ❑
   b) 'Buy two get one free' promotions ❑
   c) Placing a product on a TV programme where it can be seen by the viewer ❑
   d) Presence at a large public event (e.g. the Bristol Balloon festival (UK)) ❑

7. Which of the following would NOT be likely to be a marketing strategy aimed at 'consideration'?

a) Initiating research with your product alongside the market leader product to communicate results in the press ❏

b) Showing how your food product compares with others in nutritional value ❏

c) Demonstrating your product's reliability compared to competitors ❏

d) Each online purchase generates a voucher code for money off the next purchase ❏

8. Which of the following would NOT be likely to be a marketing strategy aimed at 'loyalty'?

a) Introduction of a customer card that gives bonuses and discounts for ongoing purchases – such as Eurostar 'carte-blanche' programme ❏

b) Reducing the price to ensure that the customer does not go elsewhere ❏

c) Member's magazine – such as Toyota's 'Club Toyota magazine' ❏

d) Collector card – Nero coffee's 'stamp' per purchase – 10 purchases permits a free coffee ❏

9. Which of the following would NOT be likely to be a marketing strategy aimed at 'advocacy'?

a) Money off your next purchase when you introduce a friend ❏

b) Viral marketing via social websites – you pass on details to your friends ❏

c) Free sampling of the product in a shopping mall ❏

d) Initiating a competition where the customer can increase their chances of winning if they give you five email addresses of their friends. You then email advising them that their friend has recommended them ❏

10. Which statement about measuring marketing effects would be the wisest?

a) Marketing is more difficult to measure than other investments ❏

b) Marketing is just like any other investment – choose what you want to happen and measure it ❏

c) Marketing is too complicated to measure using conventional techniques and so requires specialist monitoring ❏

d) Marketing cannot be measured effectively and effort doing so is usually counterproductive ❏

THURSDAY

Understand brand strategy

Brand strategy is one subset of marketing strategy. There is a lot more to marketing than just brand strategies but the emphasis, importance and power of the brand mean that brand strategies deserve a chapter to themselves.

There is no universal definition of a brand – like vision, strategy, culture, values – we all have perceptions of what we mean by a brand, but these may differ from someone else's definition of a brand. This does not aid effective communication.

A brand can be:

- an identification mark on skin, made by burning (especially an owner's identification on an animal's body)
- a fictional character from J. R. R. Tolkien's Middle-earth
- the name of a beer produced in Wijlre, Netherlands
- a play by the Norwegian playwright Henrik Ibsen
- a verb – to accuse or condemn, openly or formally, for example to 'brand' as disgraceful
- a type of sword: a cutting or thrusting weapon with a long blade
- the name of 31 separate villages throughout Germany and Austria
- a trade name: a name given to a product or service
- the sum of all the characteristics, tangible and intangible, that make an offer unique
- the immediate image, emotion or message that people experience when they think of a company or product

While the last three, above, are all perfectly acceptable, I will suggest a widely embracing definition:

'a trade name and all associated factors, attributes and messages of a product or offering'

An organization will want to enhance, develop and protect these factors. This activity is termed 'brand strategy'.

The purpose of brands

The origin of the use of the word 'brand' in this business context is from the cattle farmer's habit of placing an identifying mark on his cattle's skin, originally by burning; these days kinder paint-based methods are common, which states that the cattle belongs to a specific farmer. The individual cow or steer then 'stands out' as belonging to this farmer. Modern business branding has the same purpose – to identify ownership and to seek to ensure that the product stands out to the customer or potential customer.

Few products are identical to every competitive offering on the market. A Mars chocolate bar is different from KitKat, which is different from Toblerone. For many of us, we have a shortlist of chocolate bars we prefer and our shortlist may include these three. In each case, the owning company (Mars, Nestlé and Kraft respectively) want their product to stand out to us and, by doing so, enable them to be our choice of confectionery.

In this chocolate bar example, the three global giant confectionery companies are using their brands in three slightly different ways. Mars uses the brand for both purposes – standing out and identifying ownership; KitKat merely seeks to stand out from other rival products and has an additional prominent Nestlé logo to identify ownership; and Toblerone seeks purely to stand out with reference to Kraft's ownership of the brand in negligible small print.

How a brand functions

Identifying ownership and standing out are just the first step. The brand gives the product or service an identity, some would say even a personality. Customers are then buying into this identity or personality when they purchase the product. Their reasons for doing so could be wide, for example:

● Image: Someone may drive a Range Rover car to identify with the prestigious image of the car – the Range Rover is aspirational and expensive, by driving it I am demonstrating that 'I am successful' in a way in which driving a Tata would not.

- Service: Many people buy certain books from Amazon despite being charged a price premium – they are choosing the brand of Amazon because it consistently demonstrates reliable, rapid delivery, and security of supply.
- Quality: Large numbers of families start the day with Kellogg's corn flakes as they believe that this brand has a higher quality of product than a cheaper store own brand (or store brand, or no brand) product.

So, the brand has the purpose of ensuring that the product stands out in the eyes of the customer, that the customer therefore identifies with this brand and consequently ultimately persuades the customer to choose to buy. The brand therefore directly contributes to business and financial performance by enhancing the sales potential.

A brand has value

Interbrand makes an assessment of the world's most valuable brands each year. Coca-Cola is the perennial winner of this assessment, valued in 2011 at US$ 71.9 billion. With some demise in the standings of Nokia, Toyota and Mercedes, the 2011 ten highest valued brands were all American. The brand value assessment includes:

- an analysis of the recent historic financial performance of the company which owns the brand, and the value it is deriving for its owners (usually shareholders)
- the role of the brand, or the proportion of the consumer decision to purchase that is due to the brand
- the brand strength, or the ability of the brand to derive expected future financial earnings.

While some may want to question the techniques and measures used, these three aspects are critical to the success of any business – financial performance, the customer choice and securing the future. Note that these three considerations have respective timeframes of 'past – present – future'. Any successful brand will be achieving in all three areas and all three timeframes. However, all decisions are about the future – it is the only one of the three that we can change or affect. So if we want to increase the effectiveness of the brand, to increase its value, what (according to Interbrand) should we do? What should our brand strategies be seeking to achieve?

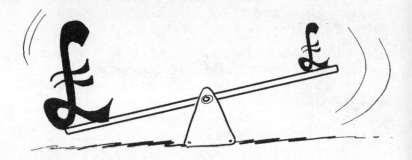

Increasing brand value

Interbrand has ten criteria by which it measures the brand strength:

Clarity

- Internal business clarity about what the brand stands for (e.g. its values and market positioning)
- Clarity on who are target customers and what causes them to choose to buy

Commitment

- Commitment to the brand from within the business and the strong understanding of the importance of the brand
- The time and investment support the brand receives

Protection

- The security of the brand (e.g. legal protection of propriety aspects, design, or geography)

Responsiveness

- The ability of the brand to respond to market changes, challenges and opportunities
- The strength of business leadership plus the desire and ability to evolve and renew the brand

Authenticity

- The extent to which the brand is based on an internal truth and capability
- It has a defined heritage and a well-grounded value set. It can achieve the expectations that customers have of it.

Relevance

- The extent to which the brand fits with customers' needs or desires

Differentiation

- The extent to which customers perceive the brand to be distinctive from the competition

Consistency

- The degree to which a brand is experienced with stability and uniformity wherever the customer encounters it

Presence

- The spread of the brand in the market and extent to which it is talked about positively by consumers in both traditional and social media

Understanding

- More than mere recognition, the brand is understood by the customers for its distinctive qualities and characteristics.

(Source: Interbrand; with some author adaptations, summaries and clarifications)

Brand strategies will therefore be targeted at enhancing these ten criteria, not merely to gain in the Interbrand standings, but to derive expected future financial performance due to enhanced sales performance. It is vital to make the link that strategies to strengthen these aspects of a brand are directly linked to future business performance and therefore future shareholder value; and the Interbrand identification and consideration of the criteria for 'brand strength' are a good way to understand this.

How brand strength is enhanced

Enhancing the brand and the earning power of the brand is achieved by increasing one or more of the Interbrand criteria. There are hundreds of possibilities for how this can be done and in the space available we will seek only to give a few examples:

Brand name: A superior brand of clothing will inform me that the article will not deteriorate after just a few cycles in the washing machine (and that wearing it will not be a fashion faux-pas); a no-frills airline brand will advise me that the flying experience will be low cost but more akin to cattle transport than any business transport to which I am accustomed. In either case, the brand name identifies and will 'tick' several of the ten Interbrand brand-strength criteria. If the clothing was inferior or if the air ticket was expensive, the brand would be damaged. If my customer experience matched, or exceeded, my expectation for that brand, the brand has delivered on its promises and strength is enhanced.

Logo: A strong identifier. I don't need to read the ingredients of my Walls ice cream to know that it will be superior to a supermarket own brand version – the logo has already given me the identifying mark of the company, which stands for high quality and therefore has also given me the expectations of the brand. Putting a Mercedes logo on an A-class or a Volkswagen logo on a Phaeton diminish the brand by reducing Interbrand's criteria of 'differentiation', 'consistency' and 'understanding'.

Straplines: UK retailer Tesco consistently states *'Every little helps'*, John Lewis consistently states *'Never knowingly undersold'*; both state that no competitor will do better. A good strapline incorporates the sales message of the brand and sums up the reason why customers should purchase from this brand. We could easily compile an A–Z of great straplines, but just a few entries from 'A':

- American Express: *'Don't leave home without it'*
- Automobile Association: *'To our members, we're the fourth emergency service'*
- Army (British): *'Join the professionals'*

In each case, the strapline added to the brand is communicating the reason to 'buy'. The Army was seeking young people to join – their 'buy' was people applying to join.

Shapes: Coca-cola have patented the shape of their cola bottle. The distinctive shape is now a unique brand communicator. To protect this aspect of the brand, the shape is patented – as should all aspects of brand communication be in order to aid Interbrand's third factor, 'protection', and seventh 'differentiation'.

Colours: Only BP can have a green petroleum forecourt, only Cadbury Dairy Milk can have their shade of purple packaging for chocolate, JCBs (UK) and Caterpillar (US) are yellow, CNN is red. Red and yellow are to DHL what brown and gold are to UPS. In each of these cases, the colour helps to identify the brand and hence enhances its strength of communication.

Smells: Identifying a perfume by its smell is an obvious requirement for a branding strategy, as is preventing any imitation, and the same is true of air freshener and household cleaning products. However, an entire industry is emerging that seeks to attach aromas to brands with the intention of enhancing memorability and strengthening the customer's ability to spontaneously remember a brand.

Sounds: 'Plink, plink fizz' is instantly Alka-seltzer. Insurance provider Direct Line has a patented musical jingle, as does Intel. The sounds enhance the brand by instant recognition by customers and potential customers.

Graphics: Pepsi has a swirl of red and a swirl of blue with a curved white line between them. This graphic serves as a logo. BP's green and yellow Helios graphic serves the same identification function. In these cases, no words are needed – the graphic comfortably identifies the brand. Other examples of graphics could include words in specific fonts – such as that of the chocolate brands Cailler and After Eight. Still others could be the five Olympic rings, KFC's cartoon-style depiction of 'Colonel' Harland Sanders, a cross or 'ichthus fish' as a graphic to denote something with a Christian emphasis.

Packaging: The toughest battles of packaging are probably fought in the perfume industry where the packaging is a major brand communicator. A walk around the perfumery section of a department store is a good education in appreciating packaging as a core pillar of branding – please do it. Chanel bottles will always be 'classic' and uncomplicated, usually in neutral colours. Givenchy will be equally uncomplicated but with bold use of strong colours. Others that want to appear less classic and more innovative will be using shape novelty and high colour innovation. Each seeks to enhance the brand by the most effective use of packaging.

Extensions: JCB earth-moving equipment is tough, rugged, durable and works in harsh environments. Their launch of a tough, rugged, durable clothing range for those working in tough environments is entirely appropriate and enhances the brand. One could never imagine soft, pink JCB-branded clothing on frail supermodels – that would destroy the brand image!

Top brands in recent years

It can be an interesting exercise in seeking to understand brand strategy to consider how brands are moving. Consider the possible causes of these movements and ask the question *'If I were responsible for that brand strategy, what would I do to enhance the brand?'* Again, this is a personal application of the learning and aims to make strategic thinking a habit for the business person.

For example, the following graph shows just a few of the highest brands over the last few years. Observe Coca-Cola as the constant number one. Ask *'What are they doing to maintain this position?'*, *'What would I do to keep that position if I were responsible for Coca-Cola?'* and also ask the negative questions *'What are the things I should NOT do? What could I do which would damage the brand value?'* An example of something NOT to do for Coca-Cola would be to change the ingredients or taste of Coca-Cola – as they foolishly sought to do in 1985 with 'new Coke'. It was a disaster and the company reverted to the original formula when customers understandably rejected it.

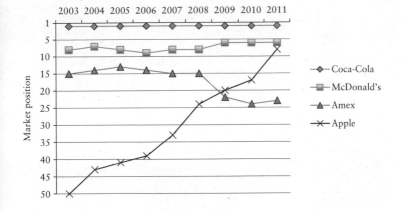

McDonalds have been consistent, Amex have fallen with the financial crisis that started in 2008 and Apple have soared as the iPod, iPhone and iPad have drawn it to prominence and profitability.

Below is a graph showing some tremendous brands with greater movement in value over the same time period. Citigroup, like Amex, have suffered since the 2008 financial crisis.

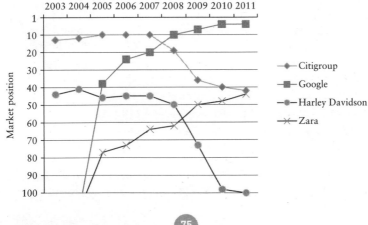

Google, Harley Davidson and Spanish clothing retailer Zara are undergoing differing but dramatic changes. Again, as an exercise in strategic thinking, recall the three key elements of brand valuation:

- recent historic financial performance
- the role of the brand, or the proportion of the consumer decision to purchase that is due to the brand
- the brand strength, or the ability of the brand to derive expected future financial earnings

With the aid of basic internet based research, identify what has happened to each, the effect you think it may have and, even more importantly, what you would do next.

Recovering from brand disaster

The graphs have shown falls for Amex, Citigroup and Harley Davidson. Decline is not necessarily disaster as good strategy can avert brand disaster and generate subsequent invigoration. A few examples:

- **Skoda:** The Czech vehicle brand was a product of the lack of competition in the formerly communist Eastern Europe and, with the collapse of communism leading to greater openness of markets, became a laughing stock and source of jokes. Volkswagen purchased a 30 per cent stake in 1991 – they had bought into what some in marketing had dubbed 'the brand from hell'. Investment, education of the workforce and taking full control in 2001 sought to rescue the brand and the first VW-influenced car was the Octavia launched in 1998. It failed. The brand had some respect in Eastern Europe but the Western European customer (especially the British) still saw the brand negatively despite the technical excellence and good reviews the Octavia received. Brand impressions are difficult to change! It had very high brand awareness, but for all the wrong reasons. The next car was the Fabia in 2000 for which the marketing parodied Skoda's poor reputation with the strapline 'you won't believe it's a Skoda'. It succeeded. 1998 research had shown that over 60 per cent of people said that they would never buy a Skoda. By 2000 this had fallen to 40 per cent; the Fabia was selling, and as a bi-product Octavia sales picked up and the previously unthinkable had happened – Skoda had a waiting list for car purchases – the brand was rescued!

- **Apple:** The US computer manufacturer was close to extinction in the 1990s with low sales levels and a low market share. The return of Steve Jobs with a new business philosophy based on cutting edge design, simplicity of use and perpetual innovation spawned a brand resurrection and in 2011 an entry into the prestigious top ten global brands.
- **Stella:** This was an iconic Belgian brand with a poor reputation in the UK due to its strength having a reported propensity for turning its consumers to violence. Its strapline of 'reassuringly expensive' inferred quality but was tarnished by extensive price promotions. In 2007, the strapline was abandoned and a lower strength beer was introduced, and later a cider ('cidre').
- **Jonny Walker:** The Scottish whiskey brand was in decline and perceived as a drink for old men. One excellent piece of insight reversed this decline – the insight that people drink whiskey because they feel successful. Whiskey says *'I've achieved'* or *'I've made it'*. The 'striding man' logo was

marshalled with the strapline *'keep walking'* and the brand has recovered.

- **Guinness:** is a classic Irish stout with an immense history. However, towards the end of the twentieth century it also had a reputation as an old man's drink and was in decline. Iconic advertising, use of the *'good things come to those who wait'* strapline and an association with the growing sport of rugby union have revived the brand.

- **Burberry:** is a clothing brand that shows the false nature of the oft-quoted adage that 'any publicity is good publicity'. Initially a high-quality quintessentially British brand, Burberry started to be popular with English football hooligans in the 1980s. This was entirely the wrong sort of customer for the brand! The 1990s saw further brand image decline as Burberry and Burberry counterfeit products became popular with 'chavs' (typically teenagers from a lower socio-economic strata). This was compounded when celebrities endorsed the brand – but a somewhat lower level of celebrity than the higher class image would want. Burberry embarked on a high-profile advertising-based strategy featuring the 'right kind' of celebrity endorsing the product and this symbol of the British upper class has now been rescued from the proletariat.

Summary

A brand has the purpose of making the customer offering stand out and be identified. In doing so, it aims to enhance the message to the customer to generate a sale. Each brand has a message – Rolls Royce's message includes being expensive, Ryanair's message includes being cheap – and it establishes an expectation in the customer of what the product experience will be like.

A brand is a valuable asset and methods of increasing the value of the brand, or enhancing its effectiveness in achieving its purpose have been summarized using the criteria used by Interbrand. While there are a myriad of other ways to do this, the method is concise and a good overview.

Brand strategies are efforts that seek to maximise the benefit of the brand and hence achieve the same objective – increasing brand value and effectiveness. Such strategies must be co-ordinated, have longevity and be targeted, as should any marketing investment.

We have also observed some brands that have risen sharply, some that are falling and some that have fallen, only to recover.

SUNDAY
MONDAY
TUESDAY
WEDNESDAY
THURSDAY
FRIDAY
SATURDAY

Questions (answers at the back)

1. What is the purpose of a brand?
   a) To make the product 'stand out' from others ❏
   b) To increase the customer's likelihood of purchasing ❏
   c) To identify the product as belonging to a particular business ❏
   d) All of the above ❏

2. Which of the following is NOT a component of a brand value?
   a) Recent financial performance of the company that owns the brand ❏
   b) Awareness – the proportion of people who have heard of the brand ❏
   c) Proportion of the customer purchase decision that is due to the brand ❏
   d) Ability of the brand to deliver future financial benefit to the business ❏

3. What is meant by the brand strength indicator of 'commitment'?
   a) Commitment of the customer to continue buying the brand ❏
   b) Commitment of the business to the brand by time and investment ❏
   c) Commitment of the company to continuing the brand ❏
   d) Commitment of the employees to understanding the brand values ❏

4. What is meant by the brand strength indicator of 'understanding'?
   a) Understanding of the customer about the brand's distinctive features ❏
   b) Understanding of the business about the importance of the brand ❏
   c) Understanding of the company about how to leverage the brand to gain sales ❏
   d) Understanding of the employees about the nature and message of the brand ❏

5. Is clothing an appropriate brand extension for the earth-moving machine manufacturer JCB?
   a) Yes, construction workers will wear the clothes and identify with JCB ❏
   b) Yes, the brand is about being tough, outdoor and rugged – these types of clothes are appropriate ❏
   c) No, the earth-moving/construction brand should not be diluted by entering different markets ❏
   d) No, companies should stick to what they do best – in the case of JCB, that is making construction industry equipment ❏

6. Why have Citigroup and Amex brand values fallen recently?
a) The companies have devoted less effort to supporting the brands ❏
b) In an uncertain financial future, they are investing less in brand marketing ❏
c) The aftermath of the 2008 financial crisis has reduced the short-term future earning potential of the businesses ❏
d) They have reduced their geographical coverage since the 2008 economic downturn ❏

7. What insight-led marketing strategy was the catalyst that started the recovery of the Skoda brand?
a) An increase in vehicle quality ❏
b) Advertising that parodied the previous poor reputation ❏
c) Manufacturing in Western rather than Eastern Europe ❏
d) Expansion of sales into Western Europe ❏

8. What insight led to the recovery of the Johnny Walker whiskey brand?
a) People drink whiskey to celebrate their success. ❏
b) The target market for whiskey is middle-aged men ❏
c) People identify with the Scottish nature of the brand ❏
d) There will always be a market for the higher-quality product ❏

9. Which of these brands has fallen in value in the last ten years?
a) Harley Davidson ❏
b) Google ❏
c) Zara ❏
d) Apple ❏

10. What tarnished the Burberry brand?
a) It was targeted as a high-class brand – this is a very small market ❏
b) It became popular with some groups of people who did not fit the brand image ❏
c) Lack of brand investment withdrew it from prominence ❏
d) Recession reduced the appeal of a high-end clothing brand ❏

Understand competitive strategy

Business is 'red in tooth and claw' as competitive organizations fight to the death for the financial favour and patronage of their customers. Any strategy a company could initiate and implement that could give them even a minor advantage, could be the factor making the difference between success and failure, between corporate life and corporate death.

In this world of cut and thrust, high stakes business activity, the temptation is therefore often to focus on the actions of the competitors. However, this, as a primary focus, is almost always a mistake. In order to succeed in this battle of business, the focus must be primarily not on the other 'players' active in the marketplace but on the customer. The customer decides the winner and loser in the market and so being preferred in the eyes of the customer is the entirety of competitive strategy. In order to do this, the wise company will, of course, have a keen eye on what competitors are doing – but only to the extent to which they are seeking to keep one step ahead in the customer's opinion, one step in favour.

This chapter will give a framework by which this focus can be maintained and, therefore, competitive strategy can be constructively engaged.

Competitive mapping

A structure I have used for many years to consider the customers' view is 'competitive mapping' (CM) (see *Strategies of the Serengeti*, 2006) – it has had a track record of providing customer and strategic insight in a vast variety of industries and competitive scenarios in many countries.

The first stage in developing a CM is to consider the market and the buying requirements from the customers' perspective – and from their prospective only. There are many circumstances when business executives hold onto opinions, convinced that '*this is what the customers think*', but empirical evidence states differently – who is correct? In all circumstances, the correct answer is that the customer's opinion is correct and many executives do not have the greatest of track records in discerning what customers really think.

I recall one series of discussions with a UK retailer who sold two distinct product categories – clothing and foods. At the time of these discussions, they were convinced that the two product types were purchased by the same customers. I was working for a supplier and we were convinced that the two product offerings had different customer groups with only a small Venn diagram overlap. The difference between the opinions was critical. If the retailer was correct, strategies could link the two product groupings. If we were correct, different strategies would be needed for each sector.

In another situation, also with a UK retailer, their customer research evidence showed that their perception of their customer was correct – but only in their geographic heartland. Customers outside the heartland had a different perspective, a different loyalty and a different set of priorities. Had they not realized this, they would have been treating all customers like the longstanding ones in their heartland – and in doing so misreading the majority of customers and undoubtedly then failing to recognize and meet the majority customer grouping desires.

Stage 1 – identify customer key issues

Stage 1 of CM is to consider the key issues that the potential customer or an existing customer sees as being important. These could be manifold. A non-exhaustive list would include:

- **product** – functionality, features, ease of use, performance, aesthetics
- **price/cost** – initial purchase, maintenance, operating, disaster scenario, replacement
- **availability** – distribution, convenience, location, speed, information
- **people** – relationship, ability, reputation, customer knowledge, service
- **technology** – ease of use, interface ability, flexibility, systems/processes, longevity
- **speed** – of service, delivery, use, time savings, productivity
- **accuracy** – reliability, consistency, error free, right first time, timeliness
- **image** – quality, brand, association, imputed image, perception
- **aftersales service/support** – speed, attitude, knowledge, function, problem-solving
- **additional offerings** – extra service, range, compatibility, offers, complementarity
- **environmental and ethical** – political, pollution, workforce, conservation, practices

- **risk** – consistency, downside, variability, security, exposure
- **flexibility** – adaptability, expandability, variability, reactivity, speed of change
- **ability** – scope, geography, skills, experience, resources

My advice is not to simply choose from the list, but to ask the question *'What is really important to our customer?'* and only then, having compiled a list from your knowledge of the customer, to use the list as a check-list to establish whether there are any aspects you have overlooked. As a tip, once we get past 12 or 15 areas to consider, the process gets a bit unwieldy, so I would recommend halting with this maximum.

Stage 2 – ranking

Having determined what is of highest importance to the customer, the second task is to rank these key issues in order of priority to the customer. The priority of the business is, again, not relevant. In competitive mapping, we only have consideration for the customer. Getting the priority wrong can lead to poor customer targeting and missing the mark with an inferior competitive offering.

This process may demonstrate that there are actually several customer groupings – several groups of people who choose to buy your product but for different reasons. One customer who makes pet dog food has identified seven categories of dog owner, each of whom has a different purchasing reason and a different set of priorities in their purchasing. These purchasing reasons tend to flow from their core reason for owning a dog. In this case, the dog food company needs seven CM analyses to maximise their ability to create the best customer offering in the market. They can then consider a co-ordinated set of strategies in the dog food market specifically targeting each initiative to the particular customer grouping to whom it would appeal. This makes each marketing or competitive initiative in the market specific.

For example, one of the groups was 'the child substitute'. This customer owned a dog and treated it like a human child. Another group was 'the security conscious', who would have a dog as a burglar alarm with an impressive dental armoury. It would be natural to assume that the two are mutually exclusive – the 'child substitute' owner is likely to have a small, cute or 'lap' dog and the 'security conscious' is likely to have a gargantuan canine monster.

The 'child substitute' owner will have his or her dog's happiness and well-being high on their list – and so would respond to initiatives in the market that target this – the highest-quality food, food that makes the dog's fur shine, food that is a treat. The 'security conscious' owner would have strength, alertness, fitness and vitality as desirable elements and so would respond positively to initiatives enhancing those attributes in their dog. The research on 'child substitute' owners shows a predominance of single women – so any advertising, promotional activity or even the design of the packaging should be with a small dog and a woman to give the 'just like me' feeling to the customer and hence appeal more specifically. The same research shows that the 'security conscious' is more likely to be middle-aged but could be a man or a woman, so someone of appropriate age should feature in market initiatives aimed here. Another category is the 'family pet owner' – clearly the dog should be shown in a family context to appeal here.

Stage 3 – self-analysis

Having determined the prioritized order of key issues for your customer, mark, as objectively as possible where your business presently sits. If the key issues are listed on the left side and a 'poor to good' scale is placed across the top, your self-analysis may look like this:

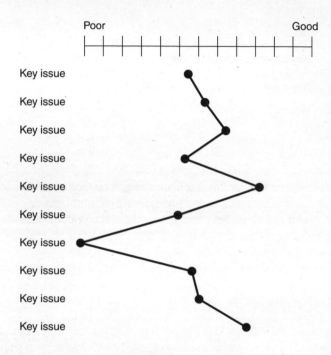

Stage 4 – analysis of competitor(s)

Having positioned your business, you may now position your competitor(s) on the same scale. Again, it is important to be as objective as possible with supporting empirical evidence.

SUNDAY

MONDAY

TUESDAY

WEDNESDAY

THURSDAY

FRIDAY

SATURDAY

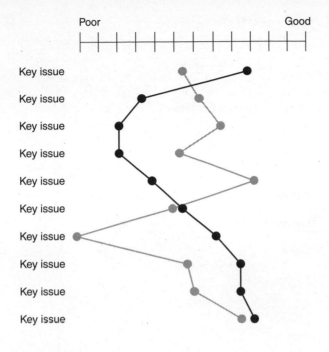

Poor   Good

Key issue
Key issue
Key issue
Key issue
Key issue
Key issue
Key issue
Key issue
Key issue
Key issue

Stage 5 – market movements

How is your market changing? The customer may be driving
a change. Many strategic analyses are static and therefore
out of date as soon as they are produced. To make this more
dynamic, the key issues can be marked with arrows to indicate
an ongoing repositioning. For example, in the fast food market,
health was previously of negligible concern. After the *Super
Size Me*[4] film and the Western obesity epidemic, the fast food
industry is having to respond to an increase in importance,
and therefore upward prioritization on the CM, of the factor of
'healthiness'.

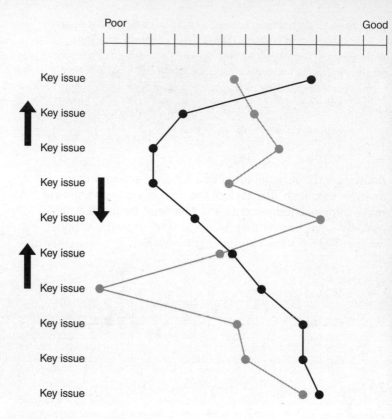

Poor   Good

Key issue
Key issue
Key issue
Key issue
Key issue
Key issue
Key issue
Key issue
Key issue
Key issue

Stage 6 – consider options

Once the competitive scenario is mapped out, a variety of options emerge:

- continue doing what we are doing
- catch up in an area where the competitor is ahead
- choose not to catch up where the competitor is ahead and seek to shift any market focus away from this area
- actively seek to forge ahead – this option can be enacted where we are ahead, level or behind a competitor
- build barriers where the competitor is behind
- seek to aggressively target the competitor by dragging them backwards – this can be where they are ahead, level or behind

- choose to do nothing except keeping a watchful eye on the competitor and re-evaluate if their position changes
- keep an eye on the market 'key issues', establish which ones are moving up and down. Keep an eye on your competitors and continually evaluate which 'key issues' they are directing their strategies towards.

Stage 7 – choose and implement

The CM analysis should produce decisions and actions. Analysis without resultant action is futile; action without analysis is foolish. The task of the analysis is to assist us to make informed judgements and to inspire better decision-making in our competitive arena, aiming to be the supplier who most closely matches and meets the customer's 'key issues'.

Illustrative example

To illustrate, let us consider a competitive scenario in the fast food retail market between competitive mapping – not a definitive statement of the competitive position of these two companies, merely an estimate for the sake of example.

Issues for a potential purchaser may be: speed of service, price, freshness of product, healthiness of the food, choice of food available, location of outlet, consistency of product on different purchasing occasions, ability to personalize the purchase through options.

Rank the 'issues'

Having identified the issues of importance to the customer, the next task is to rank them. As mentioned earlier, it is important to take time to get this right as a different rank may lead to a different competitive strategy. Remember that it may be that for different customer groupings the issues are similar but the ranking is different. It would be important to recognize this and create a competitive map for each customer grouping rather than to try to over-simplify the position with a forced compression of several persona, or customer groupings, into one artificial homogenous list.

However, for illustrative simplicity, we will have only one CM analysis.

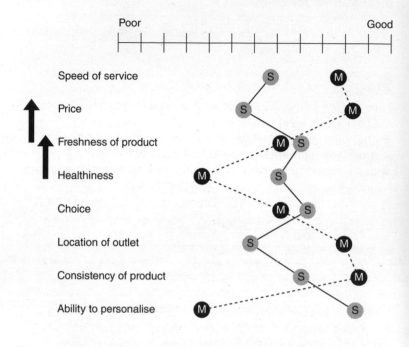

For example, presently we see McDonald's taking a range of initiatives to appear more healthy and to mitigate the negative publicity of aspects such as *Super Size Me* and the UK 'McLibel'[5] legal case, in addition to seeking to assuage concerns about obesity. They are taking a range of environmental initiatives to present themselves as a responsible global business and are actively associating with healthy pursuits. A non-exhaustive list of some of their initiatives include:

- replacing polystyrene packaging with recycled cardboard packaging
- declaring the calorific content of products
- running vehicles on environmentally friendly biodiesel fuel
- restricting 'upselling' (presumptuously asking 'would that be large?' when the customer merely asks for fries without specifying a size)
- changing the internal décor from a 'plastic'-looking red to a more environmentally-sound looking green colour
- using organically grown coffee and milk plus locally-sourced products
- working with protest group Greenpeace to ensure that the soya they derive from Brazil is from sources which do not damage the environment
- sponsoring sporting initiatives.

By choosing to consider this simplified CM analysis and to draw your own conclusions, you are not merely considering strategy theoretically – you have made the first step to actually doing it! The exercise of producing a CM analysis for any market you choose to observe and then considering what actions you would consider from your analysis is an excellent habit to start and the first step towards making strategic thinking an ongoing real-life consideration, not a mere academic exercise. It is this ability, which we will consider in the final chapter as part of a route to help you be a strong strategic thinker and therefore a valuable asset in any organization for which you work.

Summary

Competitive strategy is about seeking to gain an advantage for your product or company in the eyes of the only people who matter – the customer. One simple tool for helping with this vital aspect is competitive mapping (CM) which:

- takes the factors that the customer, or potential customer, sees as important
- ranks them in order of importance
- places your business
- places competitor business(es)
- identifies market changes
- considers options for action
- drives a choice for strategic implementation.

There are many more complex analytical tools available and CM should be seen as a complement, not a substitute for many. However, it is quick, easily understandable and also rapidly identifies knowledge gaps where we are ignorant of our consumers' opinions.

Practising completing CMs and then using the analysis to drive options for consideration is quick, easy to do and a good step towards ongoing strategic thinking as a personal habit.

Questions (answers at the back)

1. Whose view does competitive mapping (CM) consider?
a) The customer (and/or potential customer) only ❏
b) A combination of various sets/categories of existing customers ❏
c) The management of the business ❏
d) The market in general ❏

2. How should you identify the 'key issues'?
a) Select them from the template provided ❏
b) Consider which your business is focussed on ❏
c) Step 'into the customers' shoes' and identify what they would think ❏
d) Determine what the board of the business think are most important ❏

3. What factors should you consider with key issues?
a) Balancing them between 'internal' and 'external' factors ❏
b) Balancing them between management opinion and customer opinion ❏
c) How important they are to the customer ❏
d) Your ability to change them ❏

4. What would you do if your identification of key issues identified several different categories or types of customer?
a) Blend them together to generate manageable strategies ❏
b) Conduct a separate CM for each grouping ❏
c) CM cannot be used in these circumstances ❏
d) Select the most important category of customer for your analysis ❏

5. Having identified the key issues – what next?
a) Rank the key issues in accordance to what is most important to the customer ❏
b) Rank the issues in accordance with your ability to affect them ❏
c) Compare the key issue with what the management team thought ❏
d) Identify the strategies you have targeting each one ❏

6. When positioning your company and the competitor, what is the best approach to take?
a) Use gut feel and position quickly – that is usually the most accurate ❑
b) Use objective data wherever possible, make educated guesses where not ❑
c) Use objective data where possible, identify and fill knowledge gaps where possible ❑
d) Only proceed when you have definitive undisputed data for each key issue ❑

7. What does positioning an upward arrow against a key issue indicate?
a) It is of higher importance or greater priority to the company ❑
b) The market is changing and this issue is increasing in importance ❑
c) The company is seeking strategies to raise the importance of this key issue ❑
d) Competitors are focussing their strategies in this area ❑

8. If your position is BEHIND your competitor, which of these strategies is NOT a viable option?
a) Develop strategies to forge ahead and catch up ❑
b) Develop strategies to 'drag' the competitor back ❑
c) Develop strategies to change the market, minimising this weakness ❑

d) Develop strategies to focus on your strengths and ignore this weakness ❑

9. If your position is AHEAD of your competitor, which of these strategies is NOT a viable option?
a) Forge further ahead and increase your competitive advantage ❑
b) Sit back and relax – you're winning! ❑
c) Seek to 'build a barrier' – something that prevents your competitor from catching you ❑
d) Advertise the difference, making the customer more aware of your superiority in this area ❑

10. From our illustrative fast food example – what would be the LEAST wise option for McDonald's?
a) Enable customers to personalize their burger (e.g. less or more relish) ❑
b) Keep focussed on price – being the price leaders in the market ❑
c) Keep developing new strategies and processes to give even faster service ❑
d) Develop more healthy options ❑

SUNDAY

MONDAY

TUESDAY

WEDNESDAY

THURSDAY

FRIDAY

SATURDAY

SATURDAY

Keeping strategy going

You have now had six days of input about differing aspects of strategy. All of it is important and it is vital to see strategy everywhere – internal, external, marketing, brand and competitive – rather than being shunted into a siding that only considers one of these. For business effectiveness, these differing elements of strategy need to work together. Having internal strategies that are not in alignment with external strategies, or even worse conflict with them, is madness – but unfortunately many companies have such things. Having brand strategies that do not align with your competitive strategies is futile and even destructive – we have illustrated this with a few examples, we could have used many more. Holistic strategy blends all of these aspects for success in any organization – profit-oriented, public sector, charity or voluntary organizations – all should embrace a holistic strategic approach with all these aspects of strategy combining effectively.

For the seventh day of strategy, we could consider a seventh aspect of strategy. However, all good learning requires review, consolidation and practical action points to take forward. This final chapter will therefore take the points of the earlier chapters, focussing on the ongoing action that we recommend for you to develop and enhance a practice of good strategic thinking.

Sunday – Understand what strategy is and what it isn't

In Sunday's Chapter, we explored some myths of strategy, we considered the journey analogy, which is sometimes helpful albeit often too simplistic, and then Henry Mintzberg's five Ps of strategy.

There can be many applications from this chapter for each reader to take into their ongoing business lives. First, the myths:

● Strategy is not military.
● Strategy is not only for the hyper-intelligent.
● Strategy is not only for the top board.
● Strategy is not a big document.

It would probably be unwise to directly lambast those who exhibit these myths in their behaviours. However, it would be wise to understand the limitations of each myth and work to eradicate these when they are observed. For example, when middle managers are gazing adoringly at the senior board expecting a strategy to fall from the sky, don't wait for it to arrive (it rarely does) – get working on the 80 per cent plus of it that you could safely already start working on as you already know much of what you should be doing and aiming for. By acting rather than waiting for what rarely arrives, you will not fall into the trap of strategic paralysis where no strategic thinking is developed due to middle managers abdicating all strategic responsibility to the board. The board do have strategic responsibility for the organization, but that should not stop each section of the organization being able to develop implementable, well thought through strategy for their areas of responsibility. Part of the responsibility of the board is to ensure that these are combining effectively and are co-ordinated – not to dictate them.

Action 1:

Get on with it – start considering strategy now.

For the many organizations who consider strategy as a big document: understand the limitations of such a document – it can become a progress limiter rather than an enabler (recall the examples earlier in this book), it can make your strategy static, cast in stone, and therefore unable to act and react as the market, competition and business change.

Action 2:

Be aware, identify and work to positively challenge limitations in your organization such as using a strategic plan as a limiter and static, fossilic strategy.

Often, a criteria for success in business is the ability to adapt in response to changes. The alternative is the strategy of the dinosaurs! One of the examples used in Sunday's chapter was that of Hoover's inability to respond to James Dyson's bagless vacuum cleaner:

Famously fed up with his vacuum cleaner's inability to retain adequate suction, inventor James Dyson created the centrifugal action of the machine that bears his name and has made his fortune.

Dyson created 5,127 prototypes in a little over five years from his first attempt in 1978. Eventually, he had his product. He then spent the next two years seeking to find a manufacturer who would be interested. Having toured throughout Europe, he was unsuccessful. The fact that the replacement bag market was worth in excess of £100 million p.a. in the UK alone was probably a contributory factor, and as the Dyson.com website gloatingly states

'... Hoover's Vice President for Europe, Mike Rutter, said on UK national TV: "I do regret that Hoover as a company did not take the product technology off Dyson; it would have lain on the shelf and not been used " ...'

After complete rejection, James Dyson decided to press on and manufacture the product himself. Within two years, it was the UK's best-selling vacuum cleaner and has subsequently moved on to international success.

Dyson's strategy was borne out of his failure to align partners to his former strategies of selling (to Hoover) or to persuade any manufacturer to make his product. His strategy was not cast in stone – it moved quickly – whether in prototype production or in the failure after failure to develop a route to get the product manufactured.

In contrast, Hoover's strategy was to focus on its profits from vacuum cleaner bags and they failed to see the threat of the new potential competitor. They failed to move fast enough and their perspective of the market was flawed. They could have undertaken a competitive mapping (CM) exercise (see Friday) and seen the potential or they could have been so set in their perspective of the market that they were unable to look beyond their own preconceptions.

Perspective was one of Henry Mintzberg's five Ps. The second application from that chapter would be to understand the five Ps:

- plan – an intended set of actions
- pattern – a consistent behaviour
- position – a location of products in a market
- perspective – a view, opinion or stance
- ploy – a manoeuvre.

Our learning here was to understand that people use the word 'strategy' to mean all five – and that they are correct in doing so. Our challenge is to be 'fluent' in being able to speak all five of these aspects of strategy. Rather than seeing them as a maze of competing definitions, consider them as equally correct but different views of strategy.

In addition, the ability to move from one to another may take strategic discussion and thought into different, challenging, more useful directions. For example, if you were at Hoover in the early 1980s and were discussing the 'plan' of the business, you could have the ability to switch the conversation to 'perspective', challenge the established norm, consider how the domestic cleaner could be seen differently and then possibly to have taken the potential threat from Dyson more seriously.

Action 3:

Understand all five Ps both conceptually and within your own business. Analyse your own business plan, pattern, position. Be able to move work conversation from one to another to gain a different angle and a different potential.

Monday – Understand what drives strategy and what strategy drives

In Monday's chapter, we considered the 'ladder of business success' model as a structure for holistic strategy. It had:

- Rungs that ensured a seamless flow from the organizational vision to what actually happens on a day-to-day basis.
- A starting rung and starting point – for any business this is the vision, what we are here to do.
- A left upright that considers 'external' strategy concerning those external to the business – competitors, customers, potential customers and even, when relevant, other interested parties such as governments, lobbying groups, pressure groups and tax officials.
- A right upright that considers 'internal' strategy – aspects over which we have control and the need to ensure that they fulfil their primary purpose, that is facilitating the successful implementation of the strategy, to achieve the goals, to make the vision a reality. These internal aspects are factors such as structure, values, culture.

Observations about ladders include that the rungs are connected to both uprights and that the uprights are pointing in the same direction. It should be so with your organization. It will almost certainly be detrimental to your business if there is any disconnect in any area of this model or if any rungs are missing. I say 'almost', but have not yet ever, in any business on any continent, found a lack of connection between rungs and uprights or a lack of alignment of both uprights or a missing rung (which means that vision fails to percolate into action) to be a positive factor.

Action 4:

Construct a 'ladder of business success' for your organization. In doing so, you will be enhancing your strategic thinking ability, making connections between activities of the business and possibly identifying some areas that are not yet right and require consideration and action.

1. Start with the vision – what does your organization exist to do?

2. Move up the rungs.

- What are your goals (see the five suggested in Monday's chapter)?

- What strategies do you currently have to seek to achieve these goals?

- What areas of goals seem to have no strategy attached to them?

- Tactics – are these strategies broken down into appropriately sized and appropriate timeframe chunks?

- Actions – are these strategies being demonstrated in the day-to-day activity of the business?

3. Develop the left upright.

- Who are the relevant external stakeholders or interested parties?

- What is your message to them?

- Can you see this message being driven by your strategy or is there any element of it being evolved disconnected from the rungs?

- Is there more that should happen for the strategy to drive the external (left) upright of competitive, customer and external strategies?

4. Develop the right upright.

- Consider your structure, culture, organizational values – do they exist as separate aspects of the organization or are they integral facilitators for the successful implementation of your strategy?

- Identify where they are effective in this, their primary role, and where they are not fulfilling this function.
- Identify why this is the case. In many businesses, it is simply that executives have never previously thought that these are parts of holistic strategy and strategic facilitators.
- Consider other 'internal factors' – 'the way we do things around here' – possibly using Tuesday's 'building blocks'.

Having developed a 'ladder of business success', it would be worth considering each aspect to determine where it is operating effectively in your company, where it is operating sub-optimally and where the connections are simply absent.

Action 5:

Having identified both positive and negative aspects of the operation of your business through this tool, identify core required actions, consider who to communicate them to and how. One very wise boss I once had said *'I can have hundreds of people who can tell me what's wrong – I want you to be the one who tells me what to do about it.'*

Tuesday – Understand internal strategy

In Tuesday's chapter, we considered the 'building blocks of business'. These are essentially a format to consider a range of the elements contained in the right (internal) side of the 'ladder of business success'. They are not an exhaustive consideration of this right upright, as aspects such as structure, culture and organizational values are not mentioned, but they are vital elements of 'right upright success'.

The 'building blocks of business' model can be used in three main ways:

- the 'benchmark'
- the 'action plan'
- the 'excellence model'.

Each of the three have value; I have seen each bear fruit in different companies and will briefly explain the thinking behind each approach.

The benchmark

For each of the seven building blocks, consider which organizations exhibit excellence in that block. Consider what they do and how they do it. Consider what you would have to do in your industry, business and situation to learn from them and increase your effectiveness in that block.

This is what I consider benchmarking should be about – looking at who is excellent at something and imitating it. Far too much business benchmarking merely compares ourselves with others who do roughly the same sort of thing and determines whether we are marginally above average! I consider this to be mostly a waste of effort when we could be considering other industries, other approaches and learning lessons in each from the best.

The action plan

This use of the blocks is an application of the 'journey analogy' from Sunday. As part of a strategy for developing the internal aspects of the business, consider each of the blocks in turn. This makes the analysis of the internal aspects of your business more manageable by breaking it down into relevant chunks. For each block, go through the journey analogy:

- Where are we? – a realistic assessment of our present position for each block.
- Where do we want to be? – a declaration of our intended destination for each block.

- Development of strategies to take us from present situation to intended destination.
- Staging posts – what will you do by when? Short-, medium- and long-term goals and actions.

Obviously, the journey analogy has highly adaptable questions and while these four are summaries, there may be many sub-questions you need to ask within each of them.

The excellence model

This approach takes the view of the requirements for success in your industry and your environment. Consider for each of the blocks, what is required for 'top of the class' success in your industry or position. A top tip here is not to be swayed by what already exists or what you already do – top of the class in vacuum cleaners is about problem-free operation by the customer and clean houses, not about changing bags! Focus on 'ideal' and then consider the gap between ideal and reality later – no good idea has ever been developed by someone who accepts or is satisfied with the status quo!

Action 6:

Choose which of the three approaches would be the most useful for you and compile an analysis of the 'building blocks of business' for your business. Ask the awkward questions:

- Where are we strong, where are we weak?
- What vulnerabilities do any weaknesses create for us?
- Is each block strongly focussed on the customer?
- What business actions are required?

Wednesday – Understand marketing strategy

In Wednesday's chapter, we acknowledged that there is no universally accepted definition for marketing, but we introduced 'the marketing funnel' as a route to understanding marketing strategy. One of the most important factors was to understand that while marketing is more of an art than a science, it is vital to have clear deliverable objectives for each marketing initiative. These must have a clear link to the 'rungs' of the 'ladder of business success' because marketing, like any other function, seeks to implement the business strategies, which seek to achieve the goals, which seek to make the vision a reality. Marketing strategies are an integral part of the left (external) upright of the ladder. Wednesday's chapter helps us identify these clear objectives and helps us to ensure that they are built into the ladder to seek strategic success.

Action 7:

Identify as many marketing initiatives as possible that your business is currently undertaking. Identify the part(s) of the funnel on which they are aiming to make an impact. Find out their specific objectives and understand how they are seeking to achieve these.

Action 8:

Make similar considerations for marketing initiatives you see from others. Walk around 'open-eyed' – seeing marketing initiatives from other companies, particularly those in different industries to yours; and then make an assessment of their aims, intentions and where in the marketing funnel they are seeking to influence.

As stated in yesterday's chapter on competitive strategy, the habit of observing the actions of others, analysing them, drawing conclusions and then asking what you would have done differently were it your decision, is an excellent habit to build into your own self-development for increasing aptitude for strategic thinking. Good strategic thinking ability is at a premium in business and well worth the investment of your time and thoughts. On one occasion I was working with some 'high flyers' of a well-known global company. They were heads of departments and heads of small countries, who had the potential to move on to become heads of large departments or large countries. We were considering strategic thinking. I asked for their observations of what was happening at McDonald's, in a similar but more detailed way to our exploration of this company in the previous chapter. One individual had absolutely no idea as he never ate at McDonald's and was shocked that I expected him to be aware of a business he never frequented. In discussion, it transpired that he walked past two McDonald's outlets on the way to work and the same two on the way home, but as he had his mp3 player plugged into his ears, he had switched off from all useful thinking and was merely listening to music. One of his transformational applications from our time together was to open his eyes! He decided to walk to work observing strategy and only use the mp3 player to 'switch off his mind' on the way home when he was tired. I would recommend this approach – engaging your brain to consider strategy at every opportunity.

In this same group was a gentleman who visited the gym three times a week, again, using an mp3 player to 'switch off' from the monotony of exercise. He too vowed to 'switch on' for at least one of his three weekly gym visits to mentally ponder something with strategic consequences he had observed during the previous week – another great use of time – the body and brain get exercised together!

Thursday – Understand brand strategy

Again, we acknowledged that there is no undisputed definition of a brand in Thursday's chapter on brand strategies but stated that they exist to identify the ownership of a product and to make it stand out. Brand strategies are just one aspect of marketing strategies, but sufficiently important for a separate chapter to develop better understanding. As a part of marketing strategies, they too sit on the left upright of the 'ladder of business success'.

We used the framework of Interbrand's criteria for brand valuation as a basis for considering a range of actions – strategic, tactical and operational – which businesses can take to add value, or by bad actions to destroy value, in their brands. Interbrand's criteria are threefold:

● recent financial performance – a past focus
● role of the brand – the impact it has on a purchase decision – present focus
● brand strength – the ability of the brand to leverage future revenue – future focus.

As we can only affect the future, not the past, we focussed on the ten future oriented factors that Interbrand measure to determine 'brand strength'.

Action 9:

Make a note of the ten Interbrand criteria. Building on Action 8, when what you are observing relates to a brand, identify which of the criteria the strategy is seeking to influence. Critically appraise it and ask 'what would I have done?'.

Friday – Understand competitive strategy

On Friday we used CM as a process and structure to understand some strategic options available in a competitive market place. The seven-stage process took us through a process to rapidly assess a competitive position, relative strengths and weaknesses, an analysis of the competitive threat and to identify some potential actions.

We considered a CM in theory, then a simplified CM of a fast food example. The obvious action is:

Action 10:

Compile a CM of your business and that of your most threatening competitor. Various possibilities may emerge:

Does the CM analysis change your perspective of how the customer thinks or even who the customer is (you may have several different customer categories)?

- Is your business best positioned to serve and target the customer?

- What are your and your competitors' relative strengths and weaknesses?

- Who is best placed to take advantage of changes you are seeing or can foresee in the market?

- What are some possible options for you to improve your competitive position?

- To which of the five Ps do these options relate?

- Are these options congruent with the rest of your 'ladder of success'?

Summary

Good strategic thinking has a good understanding and grasp of strategic issues as a pre-requisite. These chapters should have given you every chance of pondering such relevant issues and a series of approaches and models to facilitate this. However, mere consideration is insufficient. Strategy is about action, not mere academic deliberation.

This final chapter has suggested ten action points, which aim to take the learning and make it an exercise in practical application. You do not have to be a Chief Executive to do them – anyone in any organization can complete these ten actions. Even public sector and not-for-profit organizations can do the competitive mapping – you still have competition, it is just of a slightly different nature (e.g. competition for central funding, charity donors, research funds, competition for gaining the desired staff).

Completing these ten action points, however, is just step one. Like the two examples of the 'high flyers' from the global business earlier in this chapter, the second challenge is to make this sort of thinking habitual. For your strategy of developing good strategic thinking to be ongoing, as all strategy should be ongoing, the challenge is to build these thoughts, processes and ideas into your daily work life. In doing so, your strategic thinking will be enhanced, your impact on your business will be enhanced, your value to your business will be enhanced and your career should consequently also be enhanced.

SUNDAY MONDAY TUESDAY WEDNESDAY THURSDAY FRIDAY SATURDAY

Endnotes

1   SWOT – a Strengths, Weaknesses, Opportunity, Threats analysis; a very popular, frequently completed but often misused analytical tool. For an exploration of how to use it more effectively, see *Strategies of the Serengeti* by Stephen Berry, 'Strategies of the zebra' chapter; also downloadable from www.StrategiesoftheSerengeti.com.

2   Mintzberg, H. 'The strategy concept 1: Five Ps for strategy' *California Management Review* 30, 1, June 1997: 11–24.

3   Marvin Bower (1903–2003) c.1966.

4   *Super Size Me* – a 2004 American self-made film by Morgan Spurlock, which traced his physical and mental decline over a 30-day period, during which he only ate McDonald's food.

5   McLibel case – British legal case '*McDonald's Corporation v Steel & Morris* (1997)' where McDonalds sued Steel and Morris for distributing anti-McDonald's literature. The case lasted for ten years, making it the longest case in British legal history.

7 × 7

1 Seven deadly strategy sins

- Thinking that strategy is all about yourself and ignoring the market and customers.
- Making strategy development a gargantuan effort rather than a smooth, ongoing, evolving process.
- Casting strategy in stone and limiting its ability to respond and react.
- Separating strategy from the rest of the business – 'the strategy team' who then become divorced from reality.
- Having a brand strategy or marketing strategy with a life of its own rather than one that is driven by and integrated into organizational strategy.
- Driving strategy by past experience rather than future aspiration.
- Failing to understand the military mantra 'no strategy survives first contact with the enemy'.

2 Seven best resources

- *Strategies of the Serengeti* by Stephen Berry (Neos Publishing, 2010). Further and deeper ideas on strategy with copious real-life examples.
- www.EvaluationStore.com to assist with communication, influencing others and building great business teams.
- *The End of Leadership* by Barbara Kellerman (HarperBusiness, 2012). A challenging look at how we lead our businesses.
- https://hbr.org for online *Harvard Business Review*
- *How the Mighty Fall* by Jim Collins (Random House Business, 2009). Salutary tales of businesses that have fallen and those that have survived.

- www.businessballs.com for a wealth of free-of-charge knowledge.
- Eyes that constantly observe, ears that always listen, a mind that consistently evaluates, courage that always tries and the wisdom to sometimes say 'STOP'.

3 Seven inspiring business people

- **Asa Candler** – took Dr John Pemberton's failing cola drink product, marketed it brilliantly and grew Coca-Cola into a world-beating business.
- **Sir Richard Branson** – constantly challenged established and complacent companies with competition, and forced industries to change as a result.
- **Sir Phillip Green** – consistently innovative retail entrepreneur since he was a teenager, growing to control over 12 per cent of the UK retail clothing market.
- **Alfred Sloan** – came into the strategic mess which was General Motors and focussed the business to create a multi-branded offering which had captured over 50 per cent of the US car market by the 1950s.
- **John Cadbury** – his process innovation created the solid chocolate bar and his family business went on to global success. His sons built the garden town of Bourneville for their workers – both innovators and ethical business people.
- **Bill Gates** – took Microsoft from an idea to global dominance. Gates has become a global philanthropist combatting extreme poverty and supporting healthcare.
- **Henry Ford** – transformed his market by a combination of product, process and marketing innovations, and led with drive and inspiration.

4 Seven Stephen Berry quotes

- 'There are two types of business – those who have their strategy right and those who are going out of business.'

- 'Short-termism is the enemy of success and the demand of investors.'
- 'Sometimes those at the top are the best politicians, not the best business people.'
- 'Inflexibility in strategy is as great an error as having no strategy at all.'
- 'No company journey is successful if the leaders spend more time looking at the path already travelled than the route ahead.'
- 'The primary job of Directors is to Direct – there's a clue in the title. They are not controllers, not managers, not clerks – they're Directors.'
- (*In the early 1990s*) 'Bottled water? That will never catch on in the UK.' (*To prove that we all get things wrong sometimes.*)

5 Seven opportunities

- **New labour forces** – working from home is now commonplace, but there are other less well-tapped labour forces. There are hundreds of thousands of highly qualified and experienced mums (and some dads) who do not want full-time jobs but would jump at a chance to work four hours a day 10 am–2 pm whilst their children are at school. How can our work patterns match those currently not working?
- **New ways of working globally** – chasing the sun is becoming more popular. A person starts some work in New York, finishes at 6 pm and passes it to a colleague in Tokyo (for whom it is 7 am) who progresses the work. At 4 pm he passes it to a colleague in London – for whom it is 8 am. At 1 pm he sends the completed work to New York where it is 8 am. The work has had up to 14 hours of development all during the time that the New Yorker has not been at work.
- **Riding the wave** – the surfer does not generate the wave – he rides it. Always be looking for the next business wave and catch on to it before others. In *Strategies of the Serengeti* I tell the story of Corah increasing their sales x35 in 16 years by becoming a committed supplier to UK retailer Marks & Spencer – and 'riding their wave of expansion'. Stay close to the innovators.

- **Energy** – the world demand for energy is insatiable. Fossil fuels have a limited life. New ways of generating and distributing energy will always be in demand. Technology for wind, wave, water and sun power generation is well established but comparatively expensive – there must be opportunities to develop more affordable systems, processes and structures.
- **Food** – with an ever increasing world population the demand for food increases. There is no shortage of food, just an imbalance with obesity in the West and starvation elsewhere. Food production from beef is very inefficient, from fish is more efficient and from insects is much more efficient – it will not be long before insect protein is fully accepted into our food chain – who is working on that technology now?
- **Waste** – in an ever disposable world we have overflowing landfills and a Pacific garbage patch allegedly the size of Texas. This is clearly unsustainable and so there is a demand for new technology and new solutions. Many are working in that field, many more are required.
- **Transportation** – the ability to transport material globally will only increase – vacuum packing salmon in Chile to enable it to be fresh after a long sea journey to the UK saves the cost of air transport – what other new, creative solutions can be made for foodstuffs, heavy equipment, delicate items. Delivery time by sea from China to the UK is 5–7 days – what opportunities are there to accelerate this whilst maintaining or reducing costs?

6 Seven things to do today

- Prepare a recession plan – strategies for the 'down' times are better prepared during the 'up' times.
- Ensure a realistic perception of your current position – not a flattering one.
- Have a clear aim of where you are seeking to go.
- Learn more about people – how to influence, persuade, inspire and communicate.

- Analyse every part of your marketing initiatives – what is each aiming to achieve? How are you measuring it?
- Visit www.evaluationstore.com/organisation_info.php to set up a motivation report – establish how inspired your team and company are.
- Do the assessment on www.StrategiesoftheSerengeti.com to see which strategies your organization is using and should use.

7 Seven trends for tomorrow

- Getting faster – the pace of change will only ever accelerate – move faster than the competition.
- Radical process simplification – it cannot take more than a couple of clicks to buy something or get the required information.
- Building communities – people like to belong – from LinkedIn groups to industry gatherings (virtual or physical) – form, belong, co-ordinate them.
- The twentieth century answers won't work in the twenty-first century – the old models and ways of doing things have gone (no more lifecycle curves and five forces) – live in this century.
- Increased polarization – the middle ground is being squeezed by the lower end (e.g. cheaper) and the higher end (e.g. quality) – invest in the poles not the middle.
- Specialization – in a world of identical offerings (commodities) only the cheapest will win – specialize, differentiate, focus – don't slip into commoditization.
- Customer fluidity – changing to a new supplier is just a click of a mouse – so greater effort and initiative is required to generate customer loyalty.

Answers

Sunday: 1d; 2c,d; 3b; 4a; 5a; 6b; 7c

Monday: 1a; 2c; 3d; 4d; 5a; 6b; 7c; 8b; 9a; 10c

Tuesday: 1a; 2d; 3c; 4a; 5c; 6d; 7a; 8d; 9b; 10c

Wednesday: 1d; 2b; 3a; 4c,d; 5c; 6b; 7d; 8b; 9c; 10b

Thursday: 1d; 2b; 3b; 4a; 5b; 6c; 7b; 8a; 9a; 10b

Friday: 1a; 2c; 3c; 4b; 5a; 6c; 7b; 8d; 9b; 10a

ALSO AVAILABLE IN THE 'IN A WEEK' SERIES

For information about other titles in the 'In A Week' series, please visit
www.teachyourself.co.uk